THE VARIETIES OF ENCHANTMENT

THE VARIETIES OF ENCHANTMENT

Early Greek Views

of the Nature and Function of Poetry

GEORGE B. WALSH

The University of North Carolina Press

Chapel Hill and London

© 1984 The University of North Carolina Press

Manufactured in the United States of America

Library of Congress Cataloging in Publication Data

Walsh, George B., 1946–
The varieties of enchantment
Includes bibliographical references and index.
1. Greek literature—History and criticism.
2. Poetics.   I. Title.
PA3015.P62W36   1984   881'.01'09   83-6467
ISBN 0-8078-1576-4

Both the initial research and the publication
of this work were made possible in part
through grants from the National Endowment for
the Humanities, a federal agency whose mission is to
award grants to support education, scholarship, media
programming, libraries, and museums, in order to bring
the results of cultural activities to a broad, general public.

Designed by Naomi P. Slifkin
Set in Palatino by G&S Typesetters

🔁🔁🔁🔁 CONTENTS 🔁🔁🔁🔁

THE VIEWS OF POETRY THAT THIS BOOK DESCRIBES are reconstructions, assembled from the poets' explicitly self-defining statements, and from other more pointed or diffuse kinds of evidence—diction and imagery, and the behavior of fictional poets and their audiences. I have tried to interpret diction and imagery seriously, even naively. For example, when Homer uses a single term indifferently to denote the particular "song," the "topic of song," and also the "competence to sing," I assume that he means what he says: he does not mean to say that these things should be radically distinguished. Fictional accounts of poetry require another kind of sympathetic examination, because the behavior of poets and audiences in fiction acquires meaning chiefly as part of a story. Thus, in the *Odyssey*, Odysseus's response to song in the palace of Alcinoos depends upon his personality, his past experience, and his present material condition; these things make him a special kind of audience. Homer invites us to deduce Odysseus's character from his behavior as an audience, on the assumption that we understand how audiences normally respond to song; if one wishes to identify the norm, one must know the causes of Odysseus's behavior.

I have tried to formulate an argument or a consistent point of view from each Greek poet's explicit statements, from the implicit sense of his language, and from the "normal" use of poetry in his fiction. There are constraints upon this method. It requires more material than some poets provide. Archilochus and Sappho are excluded, most notably among authors of lyric, because the extant fragments are neither copious enough nor explicit enough about poetics to support an articulated argument. Sophocles is excluded because in all his plays there is little that invites attention to theory. He was an explicit theorist—he wrote a treatise called "On the Chorus," now lost—but

Sophoclean drama, as Aristophanes realized, somehow evaded the critical controversies of the time. Its hidden principles can be formulated but not in a way congruous with the arguments presented here.

There is also a constraint upon the validity allowable to the poet's argument. His argument suggests what he regards as a desirable way to understand the nature and function of poetry; it is not reliable, of course, as a picture of the facts. It is probably true that Homeric song changed and evolved from one performance to the next, but Homer encourages us to forget this. He presents himself as he wishes to be seen, guiding his audience to an appreciation of the poem as a thing immune from human influence, an archaic repository of knowledge, timelessly preserved.

Finally, there is a constraint upon the way one explains what Greek poets say. They must represent themselves plausibly, according to the judgment of their contemporaries, and so their arguments are fitted to a context, to changing experiences and beliefs. But what is best known about each poet's context is the work of other poets; Greek poetry is a richer and more subtle index of experience and belief than anything else that remains of the people who produced it. Perhaps, then, one may begin the task of explaining what the poets say by looking simply at the logic of the texts. When the texts themselves are clearly seen, a sense of context follows.

Approached in this way, the history of Greek poetics from Homer to Aristophanes seems to be controlled by a chosen preoccupation with enchantment, the audience's emotional response to the performance of song. Enchantment is the pivotal topic in Homer's account of his art—it explains his ability to please an audience of men while preserving the gods' impartial knowledge. Although Homer's notion of enchantment raises as many problems as it solves, the poets who come later do not abandon it; they redefine it, solve Homer's problems, and successively discover new ones. The result is an orderly reworking of a tra-

ditional program for poetry, an art persistently conceived
(until the time of Aristophanes) as the medium of enchantment. The articulation of this evolving program is the principal theme of this book.

All translations from the Greek are my own.

I owe a lot to Anne Burnett, Raymond Geuss, Michael
Murrin, and Jay Schleusener, who read early versions of
the following essays. Everything here, from start to finish,
has been addressed to them. I have been fortunate also in
having, at various times, the advice and encouragement of
Geoffrey Kirk, Gregory Nagy, James Redfield, Charles
Segal, and Froma Zeitlin. My work was supported by the
National Endowment for the Humanities with a Fellowship for Independent Study and Research (1979–80) and
by the University of Chicago.

THE VARIETIES OF ENCHANTMENT

CHAPTER ONE

TRUTH AND THE PSYCHOLOGY
OF THE AUDIENCE: HOMER

⌐⌐⌐⌐⌐⌐⌐⌐⌐⌐⌐⌐⌐⌐⌐⌐⌐⌐⌐⌐⌐⌐⌐⌐⌐⌐⌐

WHILE THE PHAEACIANS IN ALCINOOS'S PALACE LIS-
ten with pleasure to the poet's song about the fall of Troy,
Odysseus covers his face with his cloak and weeps. His
tears epitomize his solitude and his oddity among the
calm, comfortable people who entertain him. Only Odysseus has direct experience of the events commemorated
in song; the Phaeacians (like us) contemplate the deeds of
heroes from a great distance, for they will never achieve
anything heroic themselves. These two audiences bring
different expectations to the performance of heroic song.
The Phaeacians feel dispassionate curiosity about distant
things they cannot know directly, but Odysseus has asked
the poet for a song about himself, to hear what he already
knows, apparently aware that his reawakened memory
will be painful. He seems almost to welcome the sensation
of grief. Perhaps the tale of his bygone triumph at Troy
strengthens his sense of himself in present obscurity; or
perhaps, having arrived once again among civilized men
and finding himself treated well by generous hosts, Odysseus falls naturally into the recollection of other comrade-
ship, with a mixed awareness of comfort and loss. For the
Phaeacians, on the other hand, Odysseus's tears make the
singer's performance unwelcome, for they insist that song
provide only pleasure, simple and unmixed, to every member of the audience. Thus, Alcinoos shows his civility as a
host by interrupting the song that celebrates Odysseus's
achievements. He can understand how a man might weep
at a story that touches him personally, but he cannot un-

derstand why a man might nevertheless wish to hear the story told.[1]

The *Odyssey*, then, contains at least two distinct kinds of audience, and both seem a little odd according to modern notions, too deeply touched by the singer's performance or too serenely pleased. Odysseus's grief seems as fresh and sharp as if he wept for something immediate and real, rather than a song about the past. The song itself, the transformation of experience into art, has not diminished the pain of recollection; no healing distance separates experience from its poetic representation. There is something almost uncanny about Odysseus's grief, for he weeps like a woman newly widowed and enslaved (8.523–30): he seems to overleap the boundaries of empathy, as if displaying a hero's magnitude of feeling. Thus, he emphasizes his special status as a veteran of Troy, a man of recondite experience and of unpredictable personality. As the man commemorated in song is special, his reactions when he hears the song are special too.

A normal audience, as we have supposed since Aristotle, nevertheless resembles Odysseus in one way: its pleasure in poetic representation somehow depends upon a sense of community with the people represented. This assumption underlies Vergil's implicit revision[2] of the story told by Homer: when Aeneas discovers, in the course of his Odyssean wandering, that the people of Carthage have painted murals representing the fall of Troy, he deduces the presence of familiar human feelings about universal human experiences; at Carthage too, as the pictures surely demonstrate, there are the "tears of things" (*lacrimae rerum, Aen.* 1.462). There are no tears for the Phaeacians, however, because they have only slight acquaintance with the realm of ordinary human "things." They travel everywhere, but in ships that guide and propel themselves: the ships, not the sailors, know the "thoughts of men, their cities and their fields" (*Od.* 8.559–61). Since the Phaeacians earn their living without effort, they excel especially in the

arts of leisure—games, dancing, music—and in this way
they seem to live like the gods, with whom they mingle
easily, as if with equals. Clearly, then, as the privileged
inhabitants of an idyllic, fairy-tale world, the Phaeacians
are exceptional. Perhaps Odysseus's tears more accurately
figure the norm for Homer's audience as well as for
Aristotle's.[3]

The ambiguity of the norm in this scene arises from a
larger contradiction in Homer's notion of his art, a contradiction that is fundamental and unresolved. There is no
third kind of audience in the *Odyssey* expressly or implicitly indicated, no middle term or common ground for
the psychologies of Alcinoos and Odysseus, and there is
no single, coherent poetics that can encompass the two audiences taken together. Rather, the psychology of each sort
of listener serves as the norm for a distinct poetics; correla-
tive with each psychology there is a different notion of
truth, for example. Such divisions within the *Odyssey* become a matter of explicit concern for the poets after Homer,
and the terms that divide one Homeric audience from
another remain the central terms of Greek poetics from
Hesiod to Aristophanes. This chapter reconstructs and
compares the two Homeric accounts of poetry, and so it
seeks to characterize at its origin a basic and abiding problematic in the Greek literary tradition.

Of the two audiences, the Phaeacians seem better established and their views seem more closely aligned with the
assumptions that each Homeric poet inherits from generations of poets before him. Odysseus excepted, all the audiences described in the *Odyssey* are like the Phaeacians in
one thing—they assume that song should provide pleasure, simple and unmixed, that there is no advantage in a
song that awakens the listener's memory of private grief.
This assumption is built into their unpremeditated habits
of speech. Thus, Eumaeus defines the singer as one who
pleases (17.385) and knows words "lovely to mortals"
(*himeroenta brotoisin*, 17.519); according to Alcinoos, the

power which Demodocus derives from the gods as a singer is, simply, the power to please (8.44f); Telemachus insists that the singer must be allowed to give pleasure in any way he chooses, as if a singer might do nothing else (1.347).

When a song does not please, of course, the singer must stop his performance. As Alcinoos interrupts Demodocus when he sees Odysseus's tears (8.538), Penelope would interrupt Phemius: his present topic "wears away at her heart" (*moi eni stêthessi philon kêr/ teirei*, 1.341f.), and so he should choose another. Telemachus accepts the principle implicit in Penelope's request, but he has a different view of its application: song need only please its male listeners, and so, if it grieves her, his mother should return to "shuttle and loom" (356–59).

The Phaeacian expectation that song should be pleasing overlaps with another pervasive, apparently traditional expectation, that singers tell the truth. The Sirens, who represent a perfect, divine type of the singer, boast of their universal knowledge (12.189–91), and they promise that one who hears them will "go away again, having taken pleasure and knowing more" (188). In this formulation, the listener's pleasure seems almost to merge, as if in hendiadys, with the knowledge he acquires.[4] According to another, more precise account, there is an aesthetically correct "shape" (*morphê*) in the poet's language that seems responsible for his listener's pleasure, but it is assumed that poetry formed in this pleasing "shape" will also be truthful. Thus, Alcinoos compares Odysseus to an accomplished singer as another way of saying that Odysseus speaks the truth; he seems to deduce Odysseus's truthfulness from the poetic beauty of his speech.

> Looking upon you, Odysseus, we do not imagine
> that you are a liar and a cheat, that sort of man
> the black earth nurtures, wide-spread and abundant,
> who fashions lies from which one would learn
>   nothing.

> Your words have beauty (*morphê*) and good sense,
> and you tell your story *epistamenôs* like a singer.
>
> (11.363–68)

If the second sentence explains the first (and there is no other explanation because Alcinoos has no personal knowledge that would enable him to detect a lie), the *morphê* and truth of storytelling do not vary independently; the presence of one indicates the presence of the other. Both qualities are denoted by a single term describing the singer's competence, to sing *epistamenôs*: the singer narrates "with knowledge" (*epistamenôs*) because he tells the truth, "with skill" (*epistamenôs*) because he tells it with perceptible beauty.[5] Among all the stories told by men, the singer's narrative constitutes the ideal, at once of *morphê* and truth.

Has the ease of Phaeacian life made Alcinoos naive?[6] Odysseus himself presumes some connection between the content of words, their perceptible form, and the nature of the speaker when he rebukes Euryalos (8.166–77). One man is physically undistinguished, but his words have *morphê*; another, godlike in appearance, speaks without grace (*kharis*), like Euryalos, who is intellectually ineffectual (*apophôlios noon*). Since each of the two possesses the virtue the other lacks, the first man must enjoy superior intellect. It is perceptible in the pleasure his audience feels in his presence, a pleasure derived from the *morphê* of his speech, but the second man, by speaking gracelessly, proves the weakness of his mind. Thus intellect and eloquence are closely bound, and Odysseus does not contemplate the possibility that a man might think well but express himself ill. To this extent, at least, he would endorse Alcinoos's notion that *morphê* and truth naturally coincide in poetry, that the aesthetically pleasing thing about song cannot be separated from the truth contained within it.[7]

Odysseus shows his difference from the Phaeacians by twisting the traditional language in which their assumptions are encoded. When he calls Demodocus's song about

Troy "too much according to order" (*liên kata kosmon*, 8.489), the unique qualification "too much" marks his critical idiosyncrasy, and the prepositional phrase "according to order" represents a traditional view of what song should be. The phrase refers ambiguously to several poetic virtues and its ambiguity reflects the assumption that song's several virtues are never encountered in isolation.

The "order" named may be of two kinds, one constituted of words and so within speech or song, or one external to speech and song. In the first case, Odysseus's use of the term *kata kosmon* suggests that he judges the articulation of song's parts as one observes a proper order in a series of ritualized actions (cf. *Il.* 24.622);[8] *morphê*, or the aesthetic "shapeliness" of the song, might be regarded as the effect of such an internal order.[9] Of a *kosmos* external to song, on the other hand, two kinds may be distinguished: first, an order of the world to which song must correspond as representation, so that *kata kosmon* would mean "the way things are." Thus Odysseus commends the singer's accuracy:

> Of all men, Demodocus, I praise you most.
> The Muse, Zeus's child, has taught you, or Apollo,
> for you sing the Achaeans' fate too much *kata kosmon—*
> all they did and all that was done to them, and every toil they endured,
> as if you had been there yourself or had heard from another.
> (8.487–91)

Every fact is faithfully represented, and the song is complete.[10] *Kata kosmon*, however, probably denotes more than the singer's accuracy: the song may be accurate and also *kata kosmon*, or accuracy itself may be *kata kosmon*. One needs a second "order" external to song, the human context of performance into which the song must fit. The song that suits a social order will be "appropriate" because it is what the audience wants, or perhaps because it is morally proper.[11]

Far from excluding one another, the three meanings of *kosmos* seem to merge in Homeric usage. If song's "shape" (*morphê*) and its "order" (*kosmos*) are similar qualities, and if verbal "shape" depends upon truth, *kosmos* in the song and *kosmos* of the world should not differ. The song viewed as an articulation of parts stands for one viewed as a representation of serially ordered facts, for the true song must reflect the world's articulation with its own.[12] *Kosmos* as social order and as the standard of truth coincide when the swineherd Eumaeus complains to Odysseus, whom he has not yet recognized, that his story about Odysseus's return is "not according to order" (*ou kata kosmon*, 14.363). Eumaeus believes the story is false and the deceit also undeserved because he has shown his humble guest kindness and was once a noteworthy person himself.[13] *Kosmos* is linked to factual, social, and formal qualities of speech in Odysseus's judgment of Euryalos: his words are false (8.179), ill-mannered, and unlike those with *morphê*; he speaks *ou kata kosmon*. Thus, the complex sense of *kosmos* as a quality of speech indicates a habit of thought like that which permits Alcinoos to deduce truthfulness from "shapeliness."

Neither Alcinoos nor Homer needs to justify his assumptions explicitly, but they might, if they wished, give a reason why the several qualities of song should not vary independently. The "shapeliness" of song indicates its truthfulness because both qualities arise from a single and indivisible competence in the poet. This view of the poet's competence, like Alcinoos's assumptions about the poem's virtues, seems to be traditional, for it can be deduced from the unexamined ambiguities of Homeric language.

When the gods make men singers, as Homer describes the process, they give them *aoidê*, "song," indifferently the product of composition or the competence to sing; between one and the other no intermediate stages can be distinguished. When Demodocus loses his sight and receives *aoidê* as compensation (8.63f.), he seems to receive a singer's ability, an occupational[14] skill, but when he performs a song about the taking of Troy, *aoidê* represents a particular piece in his repertory (8.499). These two aspects of *aoidê* merge to produce a third in another account of the Muse's gift: the poet's repertory of tales (*oimai*)[15] is what wins him honor and constitutes his competence (8.479–81); *aoidê* is a collection of songs among which the singer chooses one song when he performs (8.44f., 1.347). In any case, his skill is best described by, and perhaps should not be distinguished from, its products, for a song may be said to exist without a singer. The gods themselves can make a song of Penelope (24.197f.), which one can imagine fully equipped at inception with epic language, a plot, and a moral point, to be transmitted from gods to singers and by singers among men. In such a case, the singer will be honored because he has among his *oimai* a song of Penelope, not because he has composed one or composed one well.

If the Muse, in conferring *aoidê* upon the singer, gives the completed song as performed rather than a skill, then what we would loosely call the singer's knowledge of facts must consist in the song itself as provided by the Muse. Just as he does not compose a song and then perform it, the singer does not first learn the facts and then artfully assemble them. According to Odysseus, the Muse "taught" Demodocus (8.488) so that he recounts what happened at Troy as though he had been an eyewitness (490f.); in other words, the god has granted him *aoidê* (498), the completed song that he now performs (499). What a modern reader conceives to be "knowledge of facts" or "subject of song," in saying that the poet "knows the facts" or "sings about his subject," Homer simply calls "song." Thus, the combatants at Troy (8.580), Orestes' fame (3.204), and Clytemnestra (24.200) become themselves *aoidai*;[16] the subject matter is converted directly into poetry, without any added art.

In the same way, according to Alcinoos, if the poet has an art, it is implicit in his knowledge of fact: he sings *epistamenôs*, "knowing what" and also "knowing how" (11.368).

It is apparent, then, that Homer's notion of "song" supports the assumptions of Alcinoos: Alcinoos can assume that poetic *morphê* must indicate truthfulness because the truth in Homeric poetry comes to the poet already equipped with speech; knowledge of the facts and the language in which the facts are commemorated are inseparable products of a single competence. This competence in turn is guaranteed by the gods who teach men *aoidê*. They are the source, first, of the singer's knowledge, for they are immortal firsthand witnesses of everything that takes place among men,[17] but they are also the source of the singer's language, because the facts speak for themselves. Thus, there is no occasion for a specifically human, verbal art to make the facts into poetry. The poet's greatest claim for himself, the claim Phemius makes when his life is threatened, is equivocally a claim also for the artistry of god. Phemius boasts that he is "self-taught, and the god has made all sorts of songs to grow" in him (22.347f.).

Phemius's indifference to the contradiction between one claim and the other cannot be accounted for simply as the result of a naive psychology that ascribes the origin of all human capacities to the gods. The gods give men *polemêia erga* (*Il.* 13.727), for example, but the poet describes in detail how men put strength and skill to use on the battlefield, and the gods' role in human decision making often serves rather to uncover than to conceal specifically human motives.[18] If poetry did not differ from fighting and thinking, Homer would say more about the making of songs. One wants a more particular explanation for Phemius's equivocality, and also for its corollary, the notion that song's virtues are inseparably joined, that the singer's language is dictated by what he describes.

It is probable that poems resembling the *Odyssey* and the *Iliad* were performed by illiterate singers for generations before Greeks began to record their poetry in writing. As each singer learned his art, he became fluent in a traditional poetic language, a language wholly formed in dactylic and spondaic patterns. Like a fluent speaker of any language, the singer could produce novel statements about unfamiliar things, but he was most at ease in describing familiar things with a repertory of fixed, traditional phrases. (His language was more fixed by habit than an ordinary language because it was more difficult to produce fluent dactylic hexameters than metrically unpatterned speech.)

Singers learned the poetic language by using it, retelling the familiar, traditional stories for which the language had first been generated;[19] subject matter and diction, having evolved together, would remain inseparably joined in every singer's education. As a singer became professionally expert in fitting together traditional phrases to present a clear, convincing version of traditional stories, it might seem, even to the singer, that the story had dictated its own verbal form. Thus, the singer's competence, his firm possession of *aoidê*, would unite knowledge of fact (the "order" in events at Troy, for example), and knowledge of form (the "order" in language uniquely appropriate to its subject matter). His fluency in epic diction would make it seem that the singer had preserved the traditional story exactly, without distortion.[20] Perhaps, then, Alcinoos's notion of a truthfulness in the "shape" of words reflects the sensibility of an illiterate audience accustomed to the art of illiterate poets.

By this account, the poet's competence evades analysis in the *Odyssey* because oral poets work unself-consciously, nourished and obscured by tradition. But the tradition itself evades analysis in an oral culture, because it is embodied only in performances, at the moment when a particular singer sings a particular song.[21] Since the song is not preserved verbatim in writing or in memory, it must be newly composed again and again, and so every version of the song stands alone, in an immediate, constantly renewed relationship to the imagined facts. When Phemius describes his art, he notices only this aspect of it, the song's inevitable[22] novelty and the singer's isolation in performance: he is "self-taught, and a god has made all sorts of songs to grow" in him, but he owes nothing ostensibly to human tradition. Of course, the god who provides Phemius with his songs is the oral poet's own practiced fluency in the traditional medium.[23] Phemius cannot clearly see his tradition because he feels more vividly what he does himself. He cannot clearly see himself as distinct from his divine teacher because he does not see his tradition. It works inside him where it cannot be observed, a magical force that guarantees that the words he chooses will always be correct.[24]

The pleasure and the truthfulness jointly prized by traditional audiences can now be described more exactly. It seems most important that singers narrate the facts without omissions, so that the linguistic *kosmos* of the poem will match the *kosmos* of things. Demodocus tells "all [the Achaeans] did and all that was done to them, and every toil they endured" (8.490). This unedited and unforgetting[25] truthfulness distinguishes song from every other sort of speech about the past, because only the gods have a perfect knowledge of all the facts, and they share it with men only through the singer's medium.[26] Since the listener assumes that song (as opposed to ordinary speech) tells the whole story, he has no motive when he hears a song to look for implication—implied facts passed over in silence or implied meaning underlying the facts.[27] Since singers present the facts exactly, each narrated fact verbally fixed in its actual order, the audience has no occasion to test the narrative against any notion derived from its own experience or observation; for example, it would not test the order of the narrative against a scheme of causes and probable effects. (This means that it perceives the truth of song directly in song's verbal "shapelessness," as Alcinoos suggests.) Finally, since all facts have the same claim to commemoration in song, they should also make an equal claim upon the listener's attention; ideally, nothing will be invested with a greater weight of feeling than anything else, and the narrative will unfold smoothly, without provoking the listener's sensibility.[28]

According to this hypothetical scheme, the exactness required by Homer's traditional poetics, the singer's fluent presentation of the facts "according to order," invites an impersonal and passive response from the audience; it calls upon nothing in the listener's own experience or knowledge, and it discourages active judgment and interpretation. As the truth of song differs from the truth of ordinary speech, the listener's experience of song will be radically different from his experience of daily life.[29] It is not surprising, then, that for most audiences described in the *Odyssey*, the pleasure song gives seems by definition to consist in the listener's unconsciousness of himself and his present situation. Homer would call this mental state "enchantment" (*thelxis*). Phemius's songs are "charms" (*thelktêria*, 1.337); the divine singers, the Sirens, enchant men with their song (*thelgousi*, 12.40, 44).[30] Odysseus, compared to a singer by Eumaeus, enchants men with his stories (17.514–21); hearing his bardlike eloquence, the Phaeacians are "possessed by a spell" (*kêlêthmôi d' eskhonto*, 11.334 = 13.2).

The charm worked by things other than song is often deceptive or destructive: by giving pleasure, enchantment makes men neglect their advantage or their purpose. Thus, Penelope charms the suitors with dissembling, "sweet" words (*thelge de thumon/ meilikhiois epeessi*, 18.282f.), and Calypso seeks to persuade Odysseus to remain with her, charming him with "soft and flattering words" (*aiei de malakoisi kai haimulioisi logoisi/ thelgei*, 1.56f.) so that he will forget his home; Aegisthus charms Clytemnestra with words (3.264) and so makes her forget her duty to her husband.[31] When the gods charm human beings, the effect may be mortal: they take from Penelope's suitors, for example,

their knowledge of self-preservation (16.297f.).[32] As enchantment is dangerous in every other instance, it can be
dangerous also when it comes from song. Thus, the Sirens'
song is deadly in its charm, apparently because it brings
men so much pleasure they forget to live.

The death one suffers in hearing the Sirens' song exag-
gerates but also typifies the charmed state enjoyed by the
human singer's audience. The Sirens' deadliness shows
that one cannot normally learn the exact and unforgotten
truth preserved by gods without sacrificing something
else. Specifically, the human singer's audience, like the
dead, have abandoned purposeful effort and the direct experience of joy; they find an enchanting truth in song, a
truth that does not address their personal feeling or satisfy
their needs, to which they respond with impassive fascina-
tion. In the underworld, there is a similar balance of loss
and gain. When Odysseus attempts and fails to embrace
his mother's shade, she tells him that he has not been "beguiled" (*apaphiskei*, 11.217) since her insubstantiality is a
normal condition of the dead. Implicitly, of course, the
shade beguiles Odysseus by the standards of living men;
there is an emptiness and a distance in things of the underworld as in all enchanting objects. (For this reason, it is
equally inappropriate to weep at a song and to embrace a
ghost with affection.) On the other hand, like singers, the
dead always speak the truth (11.148).[33]

The separation of song from the active experience of life
is represented at a more mundane level in the *Odyssey* by
the social position of singers and singing. The singer is a
public figure, a *dêmioergos* like a seer or a physician (17.380–
87), and as such he does not belong to the household for
which he sings. He seems always to be an outsider (*xeinos*,
17.382), less attached to his patrons than even a seer, for
the gods are his audience as well as the source of his skill
(22.344–49; cf. 312–25). This is especially a matter of pride
for Phemius because he wishes to dissociate himself from
his human audience: his art, he suggests, cannot have

been touched in any essential way by the crimes of the suitors, who forced him to perform.[34] The professional singer does nothing but sing,[35] and so Demodocus's blindness seems paradigmatic in barring him from any other activity or sensation. For the audience, the performance of song stands apart from the feast as a somewhat formal occasion,[36] ideally to be kept free from distraction. Those who place themselves too much in this sphere are thought idle, like Penelope's suitors (1.158–62), or at least extraordinary, like the Phaeacians, who earn their living so easily (7.114–32, 325f.; 8.557–63) that they count music and dance among their principal occupations (8.244–49). Thus, as the singer does not engage in the activities of other men, other men usually regard their enjoyment of song as an experience without purpose or worldly consequence.[37]

This seems to be the traditional view of poetry in the *Odyssey*, the view required by antique assumptions about the competence of poets and the special kind of truth that poetry preserves. Song can make no appeal to the listener's sense of purpose because its chief effect is "enchantment," the suspension of self-consciousness and personal feeling. Enchantment is an effect, perhaps, of song's unedited truthfulness: the facts commemorated impartially compel the listener's impartial attention.[38] Audiences perceive truthfulness in the "order" of poetic speech, an impression produced by the singer's fluency in making and remaking the story for each performance. His fluent truthtelling seems unearthly, the product of a divine skill that binds the singer to the gods and exempts him from the forgetfulness and the partiality of men.

None of these rules applies to Odysseus. Song does not enchant him—he is not impassively pleased by its exact, divinely preserved truthfulness—and therefore he does not treat poetic art as self-validating or self-contained, something to be judged apart from experience or present need. Odysseus most clearly shows his difference from the traditional audience by treating "orderly" truthfulness as an equivocal virtue. Demodocus, he says, has told the story "too much according to order," and so it seems that Odysseus would prefer another kind of song, one that does not recount "all that the Achaeans did and all that was done to them" (8.487–91). He wants something particular and personal, a song about himself and his contrivance, the Trojan horse. Therefore, he asks Demodocus to sing not *kata kosmon*, following the "order" of the Trojan story as a whole, but *kata moiran* (8.496), giving the part its due.[39]

A performance that commemorates the listener to himself will not enchant him—enchantment is a kind of unconsciousness. Perhaps, since the song Odysseus requests describes a time of triumph (520) and good fellowship, it might have made him feel simple pride or at worst a quiet nostalgia. (Demodocus's first song, by contrast, described a quarrel with Achilles [8.73–77].) His weeping indicates, however, that Odysseus construes what he hears in relation to some present trouble, that his present unquiet condition, more than the topic of the song, determines his response as an audience. (Thus, Eumaeus can contemplate his troublesome past with equanimity [15.398f.] because he has become reconciled to the present; when Odysseus has killed the suitors, he too enjoys the tale of old adventures [23.300f.].) Like Odysseus, Penelope construes the song she hears in relation to her present condition: she misses her husband, and the story of the Achaeans' return makes her feel his absence more sharply (1.340–44). When she responds in this way Penelope "joins" the song with her thought (*phresi suntheto*, 1.328): the process can be called *synthesis*. It is a normal response in ordinary conversation, in which each participant weighs and interprets the other's words to find their bearing upon himself; *synthesis* is the listener's effort to grasp what the speaker means, the point of his speech.[40] The singer's audience, of course, does not normally make this effort, because the singer, according to traditional rules, does not mean to say anything of present or personal significance.

When Odysseus asks Demodocus for a performance in which, it seems, *synthesis* will be the goal and "orderly" truth an impediment, he makes the singer's art into something like the storytelling that Telemachus hears at Sparta. There, at dinner in the palace of Menelaus, Helen promises a tale suited to her audience (*eoikota*, 4.239),[41] a tale about Odysseus that will please his son. She will not name all the man's trials, but only one, typical of the rest (*hoion tod'*, 242);[42] when she has finished, Menelaus praises her for having spoken in the way that Odysseus wants Demodocus to speak, *kata moiran* (266; cf. 8.496), giving the part its due and so capturing the special quality of the man she commemorates (267–70). Evidently, Helen's performance allows greater weight to some facts than to others because the listener's perspective must be taken into consideration and also because she wishes to present something other than facts. There is a pattern that the listener must infer from the story, and in this pattern a point to be grasped. Thus, Menelaus praises Helen's story because it correctly represents (by mimetic synecdoche, taking the part for the whole) the kind of thing Odysseus did, and he can make this judgment with confidence because he knows the rule that defines the category: he knows Odysseus's "heart" (*kêr*, 270f.), an internal quality, the governing principle of the man's behavior. Perhaps, then, the point of the story has something to do with the "heart" of the hero.[43]

There are two liabilities in poetry conceived on the model of Helen's storytelling and the song that Odysseus solicits from Demodocus: nothing in the words themselves can guarantee either the listener's pleasure or the speaker's truthfulness. *Synthesis* is clearly inimical to enchantment, which protects an audience from painful self-consciousness, and so the singer who appeals to *synthesis* risks enhancing his listener's pain.[44] Therefore, to make her story pleasing (239) and *synthesis* endurable, Helen must use another art, Egyptian pharmacy: she puts a drug in the wine, a drug that can stop a man's tears even if he watches with his own eyes the violent death of his brother or his son (223–26). The drug works a compromised sort of enchantment, dissolving emotion but leaving consciousness intact, so that the audience remains interested in the story's point. If words alone could do this, *synthesis* and enchantment might be reconciled. The drug is necessary because stories like Helen's are essentially painful, and this means that words with a point cannot soothe the people who understand them.

The truthfulness of words with a point is questionable because one cannot be sure that the pointed story, true as to type, is also true in detail, and this is especially troublesome because the quality that makes a true speech pointed makes a false one plausible. Before he has been recognized by Eumaeus, Odysseus tells him a false tale which celebrates the deviousness and the generosity of Odysseus at Troy. Because Eumaeus can see that the point of the tale is correct, that it represents correctly the kind of thing Odysseus did, he believes the lie, and he praises the liar much as Menelaus praises Helen, for "not failing to give the part its due" (*oude ti pô para moiran*, 14.509; cf. *kata moiran*, 4.266, 8.496). Eumaeus believes most of another false tale—Odysseus "provokes his heart" with sympathy (14.361f.)—but he rejects one detail, despite his sympathetic impulse of belief, because he supposes that he knows, in the single instance, what actually happened. In accordance with his feeling, Eumaeus might have called the story *kata moiran*: his belief is a function of the heart, and his heart responds because it recognizes the type of human misfortune, in which one man's trouble connotes another's. Judged against the standard of his knowledge, however, the story seems to distort the "order" of events, and so Eumaeus calls it "not *kata kosmon*" (363).

Although Odysseus is not a singer in the *Odyssey*, his storytelling art is like a singer's, and this is the way Alcinoos and Eumaeus praise him (11.367–69, 17.518–21; cf.

21.404). At the same time, as a storyteller, he has a natural affinity for deceit (13.293–95). Homer does not explicitly suggest that singers may therefore sometimes deceive their audiences, but he has certainly made the inference inevitable for the later tradition. Thus, because Odysseus tells "lies that resemble the truth" (*pseudea . . . etumoisin homoia*, 19.203), Hesiod's Muses also tell "lies that resemble the truth" (*pseudea . . . etumoisin homoia*, *Th.* 27).[45]

As the problem first takes shape in the *Odyssey*, two sorts of truth are available to poetry: the "orderly" and enchanting truth, which is always pleasing, and a selective, pointed truth, which seems inevitably disturbing. By juxtaposing them, the *Odyssey* raises questions about both. There is a danger in enchantment, which the Sirens exemplify, for the victim loses all awareness of himself and thus all power of judgment; enchanting poetry compels an absolute faith in the poet's integrity. (The pointed story, by contrast, appeals to the listener's experience, his developed sense of the actual and the possible, and so he can judge the pointed story, however fallibly.) Therefore, if the poet enchants, as Odysseus enchants the Phaeacians, and lies, as Odysseus lies to Eumaeus,[46] his audience will be defenseless. Alcinoos's trust in Odysseus, the traditional attitude of the poet's audience, begins to seem misplaced. For Hesiod, who wishes to work spells like the traditional singer in the *Odyssey*, but in the absence of traditional assumptions of truthfulness, it becomes necessary to confront the danger of enchantment and deny it. He must somehow assure his listeners that enchanting poetry (his own, at any rate) is truthful and benign. On the other hand, in poetry such as Pindar's, which is fashioned with a point to quicken the listener's self-consciousness, it is the point that needs justifying. An aesthetic problem is already apparent in the *Odyssey*; it is embodied in Odysseus's tears, his response to the song about himself. There is a moral problem as well once Homer opens the way to selection and judgment as elements of the poet's art. If he no longer tells the "orderly" truth, the poet ceases to be impartial, and in his partiality he becomes implicated in the life of ordinary men. Thus, Pindar will assert what Phemius would deny, his responsibility and his responsiveness to others: the poet can corrupt an audience, and the audience can corrupt a poet.

CHAPTER TWO

TRUTH AND THE PSYCHOLOGY
OF THE AUDIENCE: HESIOD

HESIOD INHERITED FROM HOMER A REPRESENTATION
of the effect of song upon an audience and of the purpose
song serves. Song pleases and enchants its listeners,[1] takes
them out of themselves, and loosens their grasp upon experience in a process that resembles more dangerous kinds
of beguilement, for example, the confusion of a soldier
who forgets to defend himself in battle.[2] Thus, the Sirens
practice the singer's art carried to its natural limits, for their
pleasing song is deadly in its charm. On the other hand,
the audience values truthfulness in the singer and seeks
knowledge from his song.[3] The Sirens claim to provide this
too, by reporting everything that occurs among men (*Od.*
12.189–91). Homer seems to notice that there is something
peculiar about an art at once informative and confusing;
his sense of a problem can be measured in the attention he
pays to Odysseus as an exception, an unbeguiled audience
and a deceptive storyteller. For Hesiod, the behavior of
Odysseus has become problematical in turn, but Hesiod
has a new set of categories for describing the effects of poetic art, categories that clearly distinguish bad spells from
good ones and false from truthful poets. Thus, he can distinguish himself from the deadly Sirens, on the one hand,
and from deceitful Odysseus, on the other.

Hesiod has renamed enchantment (*thelgein*) as forgetfulness (*lêsmosunê*)[4] and the retention or acquisition of knowledge as memory (*mnêmosunê*). In his paradoxical account of
the Muses' parentage and function, the two conflicting

terms are coordinated by their sound, rhythm, and position in the verse:

> Mating with their father, Kronos' son,
> Memory, who rules the hills of Eleuther,
>   bore them in Pieria, bore
> forgetfulness of evils and a rest from cares.
>
> (*Th.* 53–55)

How, the reader is invited to ask by this formulation, can the same goddesses at once be the children of Memory and the bringers of forgetfulness? This is Hesiod's version of Homer's view that truthful songs disorient their audience.

The forgetfulness that song brings is described at greater length a little later in the poem:

> If a man has reason to grieve, and dries out his heart
> troubled with the spirit's fresh pain, yet the singer,
> the Muses' servant, sings the famous deeds of
>   bygone men
> and the blessed gods who hold Olympus,
> at once the mourner forgets his grief and
> remembers none of his cares; but swiftly
>   the goddesses' gifts divert him.   (*Th.* 98–103)

In both passages the audience is made to forget its troubles (*kaka, kêdea, mermêrai, dusphrosunai*), and in the second one finds that it is reminded of the accomplishments (*kleea*) of earlier generations and of the immortal gods. Memory of these remote things is the index of song's ability to inform, but, because it supplants the listener's memory of himself, it also explains song's ability to induce forgetfulness. Hesiod's new names for the knowledge and beguilement in Homeric song therefore allow him to specify their mode of action in such a way that they may function together coherently: memory and forgetfulness govern different objects, the first what is far away,[5] the second something personal and painful. One effect requires the other, and song fails if the wrong sort of memory is awakened. When Odysseus weeps at Demodocus's song of his own past life in the eighth book of the *Odyssey*, he obtains, according to a traditional view, neither the proper sort of memory nor the desired sort of forgetfulness; his response to song makes an exception that proves the psychological rules of performance, for Hesiod as well as for Homer.

Hesiod preserves the link between knowledge and pleasure by which poetry is characterized in the *Odyssey*. The Hesiodic Muses regularly sing beautiful songs: their voice is sweet (*Th.* 39f.; Calliope is foremost among them, 79), lovely (65, 67: del. Wolf), and delightful (68). Like the Homeric bard, they please by informing their audience (*tai Dii patri/* . . . *terpousi megan noon*, 36–38), and when Hesiod asks the Muses to report through him the generations of gods, he asks also for "lovely" or "desirable" song (*himeroessan*, 104; cf. *Od.* 1.421, 17.519).[6]

But the notion of a pleasing truth or knowledge does not control the Hesiodic account of song so directly as it does Homer's.[7] Odysseus is compared to a singer in the *Odyssey* because he tells the truth and tells it with a "shapeliness" (*morphê*) in his words (11.367f.); both his truthfulness and verbal skill may be denoted by a single qualification, that he speaks *epistamenôs*. Odysseus himself distinguishes ugly falsehood from speech that pleases its audience "without fault" (*asphaleôs*, 8.171); there is a single "fault" in speech, an error coincidentally of fact and of style. When Hesiod borrows these terms to draw a comparison between singer and speaker, the question of truth becomes less important. Hesiod's king, like a poet, derives his skill from a Muse (*Th.* 79f.); his words flow sweetly (84) and he speaks *asphaleôs* (86); he resolves quarrels and delivers judgments *epistamenôs* (87). But *asphaleôs* need not mean "without error of fact" or "truly" here,[8] and *epistamenôs* more probably signifies the king's competence to render just decisions (85f.) than skill in true speech. The king's two skills come from different sources: he is a king, and so just, "from

Zeus" (96), but he speaks sweetly with the help of Calliope. Since his eloquence does not arise from his justice, it
seems to connote nothing beyond itself; it is neither a
symptom of the speaker's accuracy nor of his propriety.
Thus, the king's art does not necessarily unite fact and
form like the Homeric singer's, and one cannot deduce his
truthfulness directly from the beauty of his words as Alcinoos deduces truthfulness in the speech of Odysseus
(*Od*. 11.363–68). Worse still, although the king who is
"from Zeus" may be both eloquent and just, the singer
"from the Muses and far-shooting Apollo" (*Th*. 94) need
apparently be nothing but eloquent.[9] If the singer's truthfulness is not evident in his language, one must look for it
elsewhere.

Among the audiences named by Hesiod, there is only
one whose pleasure necessarily depends upon the singer's
truthfulness. The Muses delight "the great mind of Zeus"
(*Th*. 37), which cannot be deceived (*ouk esti Dios klepsai
noon*, 613; cf. 656). This god therefore seems a special case:
he is like Odysseus, whose direct and personal knowledge
of the singer's theme distinguishes him among the human
audiences of the *Odyssey*. Although other Homeric and
Hesiodic audiences take their pleasure from the beguilement or forgetfulness worked by song, Odysseus and Zeus
do not, for in knowing beforehand what the singer celebrates, they can never be seduced from self-consciousness
or from knowledge. Zeus must discover himself in the
song which Hesiod sings about the generations of gods
and the god-given achievements of men (cf. *WD* 2–4),[10]
just as Odysseus discovers himself in Demodocus's song
of Troy.

The truth makes Odysseus weep, but it delights Hesiod's
Zeus. The god's pleasure suggests that his response to
song is governed by rules wholly different from those governing the response of human audiences in both Homer
and Hesiod. Song's truth makes the knowing Odysseus
weep because it fails in its purpose, but it delights a know-

ing Zeus because it succeeds. Since Zeus evidently enjoys song without experiencing forgetfulness of any sort, song's success on Olympus must depend upon qualities other than those necessary among men. Human audiences differ from Zeus in experiencing forgetfulness in song as they differ from him in their vulnerability to deception. Thus, there should be two sorts of song for Hesiod as there are two distinct audiences representing different norms of response. Zeus's unique status and the Muses' true song that he hears will distinguish by contrast the condition of the human audience and the nature of the human singer's art.

The Muses explicitly claim to sing two sorts of song (*Th.* 27f.). One, which is true, must be what they perform for Zeus and perhaps for others. There is a second sort, however, different from true song, for which human beings are the only conceivable audience. Although Hesiod does not explicitly say that the Muses sometimes sing truly to men, he suggests that they often sing falsely, and their falseness points to the fundamental problems of Hesiodic art. It makes a difference, according to Hesiod, which kind of song the Muses sing—he wants his own poetry to be truthful (cf. *WD* 10)—but it is not clear what the difference might be. What particular sort of truth does Hesiod look for, and how, in the experience of his audience, will the true song of the Muses differ from the false?

The first of these questions has two answers because there are two ways to read the Muses' boast:

> We know how to make many false statements that
>   are like[11] true ones [or real things],[12]
> but when we wish we know how to tell the truth.
>
> (*Th.* 27f.)

According to one interpretation of this passage, lies are like "real things" (*etuma*); according to the other, lies are like "true speech" (*etuma*). Each sort of falseness entails a different notion of the truth.

If lies are like "real things," and if these things are the

subject of the song, it seems possible that an audience can learn something from the Muses' lies since the likeness of lies and facts suggests that lies are only partly deceptive. On the other hand, the audience must also mistake something essential in the facts song professes to represent. Its mistake arises from the Muses' success in commanding belief by making their lies resemble what the audience already knows from experience. Thus, the likeness of lies and facts in song (*pseudea . . . etumoisin homoia*) would best be named plausibility. In casting the Muses as both imperfect informants and successful deceivers, Hesiod takes as his model the storyteller, Odysseus, rather than the bard in the *Odyssey*.[13] The Homeric bard, Odyssean audiences assume, will tell the truth if he knows it, and the more he knows, the better a bard he will be. Odysseus and the Hesiodic Muses, on the other hand, know more than others but often prefer to lie, as if their knowledge made them jealous of the truth. If the Muses lie as Odysseus does when he promises Eumaeus and Penelope his own imminent return, with stories that are false in detail but true in substance,[14] their deceptions perhaps offer men knowledge, at least knowledge of the dissembling and opaque sort generally associated with oracles. But they may also lie as Odysseus lies to his enemies, with stories true in detail but false in substance,[15] so that the real things reflected in their fictions serve merely to seduce and destroy their listeners.

It is not clear how song reflects real things falsely. Hesiod can scarcely mean that all song is imperfectly mimetic, distorts the world in representing it, and for that reason deceives us, because the Muses sometimes sing the truth, not "lies like real things." Do the Muses therefore achieve a perfect mimesis when they sing the truth, and lie about the world by distorting its image? One would expect a perfect mimesis to produce the same effect upon its audience that reality itself does, and so Hesiod's Muses would anticipate by centuries Gorgias's account of art in the *Helen*. For

Gorgias, spoken words (*ta legomena*) and paintings are somehow like (*homoia*) the persistent mental impressions made by such real things as the sight of an enemy in armor upon the battlefield. They are alike in disturbing the soul (*psukhê*) and in driving thought (*phronêma*) from it because the natural mechanisms of human psychology do not distinguish between real things that are present and the memory, anticipation, or artistic representation of them.[16] If the Muses' lies are like (*homoia*) real things in this sense, poetic fiction mimics life in awakening the same feelings as actual experience.[17]

Although Hesiod does not reveal what effect the Muses' fictions produce upon their listeners, or how often the Muses lie, what he does say about the psychology of audiences makes it unlikely that the true song should imitate life. The effect of song differs from ordinary experience: song brings forgetfulness, relief from the emotions evoked by mundane cares, just as Homer's song beguiles its listeners and relieves them of self-consciousness.[18] The distinction between present and absent, between experience and the subject of song, is therefore essential to the Homeric and the Hesiodic praise of art. Without it, song would offer no advantage over life, and the fearsome or grim stories it tells would frighten or grieve the audience as much as actual danger or pain. The audience of Hesiod and Homer looks to art for the truth but not for the actual or the real.

This rule holds true even for the *Works and Days*, although everyday human experience is the poem's subject matter; thus, it seems true a fortiori of the *Theogony*, a poem about the gods. The *Works and Days* is based, of course, upon the poet's practical knowledge, and it is meant to be useful as a guide in the active pursuits of life. But as a poem, a thing given by the gods,[19] performed by a singer and appreciated by an audience, it is distinct from life. Its utility depends upon its power to interrupt its listeners' patterns of behavior and to make them perceive what the god or the singer wishes rather than the "facts" by which they are otherwise motivated. For the poet of the *Works and Days*, it is a fundamental condition of the practical life that its successful pursuit lies beyond the experience of men, hidden by the gods as punishment for Prometheus's treachery (42). This may be perceived only by those who draw back from what they know directly and from motives, such as greed, that are tied to known, desired things.[20] If men do this, they learn that "the half is more than the whole" (*pleon hêmisu pantos*, 40). Hesiod himself has learned by rising above the shepherds, who are "bellies only" (*gasteres oion*, *Th.* 26).

Thus, if one follows the implications of "lies like real things," the Muses warn men against lies precisely because lies resemble real things, the things that happen in the daily course of life. Their resemblance to reality makes them plausible or realistic, and therefore doubly dangerous. They are not true (*alêthês*), however, for the truth is something normally hidden from men, something that has been rescued from concealment by the art of the poet with the help of the gods.[21] The Muses' boast at the opening of the *Theogony* may then serve as a particular justification of that poem, an invitation to discover the truth, beyond experience, in the poem's remote cosmological abstraction.

By making his Muses sing "lies like real things," Hesiod elicits new meaning from the Homeric description of epic performance. In the *Odyssey*, true song enchants because it weakens the listener's grasp upon the real things surrounding him. It may therefore have seemed true to Hesiod because it enchants, true to the extent that it sets absent objects—past or future, divine or fabulous—before present, tangible ones in the listener's mind. If the truth is located at a distance, realism, which must always be defined in terms of the present and the tangible, begins to seem false. But since Hesiod's truth seems recondite only because it lies beyond the experience of his listeners, his Muses may, when they wish, sing truly, and the poet acknowledges no fundamental inadequacy in his verbal part.

Nevertheless, since the expression *pseudea etumoisin homoia* does not unequivocally signify "lies like real things," the chain of inferences drawn from this translation risks straying progressively farther from what Hesiod or his Muses wish to tell us. The word *etuma* by itself can scarcely signify a disparaged, banal realism, and one cannot prove from the usage of Greek authors that *alêtheia* refers to a quality of things rescued from concealment (*Unverborgenheit*).[22] Only this much seems clear: song will succeed best for the audience Homer and Hesiod describe if its truth consists in the distant and unfamiliar; the poet who knows this has been set apart from other men.

The alternative reading of the Muses' boast requires another account of Hesiodic truthfulness. If one renders *pseudea etumoisin homoia* as "lies like true speech," one assigns a different sense not only to *etuma* ("true speech" rather than "real things") but also to another key term. Lies are "like" (*homoia*) real things as a representation resembles its model, but they must be like true speech in some other respect. Thus, two sorts of deception may be distinguished: one, which works by manipulating "facts," recalls Odysseus's skill at constructing likely stories, assembled from elements of his experience but somehow distorted in the process; another succeeds by purely verbal manipulations, so that the words of lies resemble the words of true speech.[23] According to the present hypothesis, the Muses claim this second, verbal skill.

By isolating his verbal skill from the singer's treatment of facts, Hesiod distinguishes himself from Homer and looks forward to the concerns of a literate age. Since *aoidê* indifferently signifies "song" and "subject of song" in the *Odyssey*,[24] the Homeric singer's art seems to encompass principally a mastery of subjects. The singer is praised because he knows what happened (*Od.* 8.489–91). His words have beauty (*morphê*) only when they are also accurate (cf. 11.363–68), so that truthfulness or the story itself rather than the singer seems responsible for his verbal skill. The story comes ready-made for singing, its verity assured because it cannot be contrived by a human being who assembles words according to his own uncertain imperatives. Thus, to the extent that the verbal medium is noticed by audiences, it must be considered as invariant as the facts themselves,[25] and Homeric song will not become attenuated with the passage of time and the multiplication of performances. Every performance perfectly matches words and story because it is directly and completely derived from the immortal knowledge of the gods. In this respect, song is superior to mere *kleos*, a report of events not couched in the divinely provided verbal and musical forms of poetry[26] and so subject to distortion.

Hesiod's Muses bring song to the level of *kleos*, for their "lies like true speech" deny the singer the divinely guaranteed coincidence of truth and poetic language upon which he relies in the *Odyssey*. On the contrary, if they stand metaphorically for human singers, the Muses make verbal skill an independent and equal partner to truth in the singer's art[27] and claim an equivocal control over the words of their song. Since the story itself no longer dictates the form in which it is transmitted, Hesiod's poet must consciously contrive his words. As he becomes aware of his contrivance, he may also begin to regard himself as unique. The Muses' lies and Hesiod's naming himself in his work (*Th.* 22, e.g.) appear to be symptoms of the same post-Homeric self-consciousness.[28]

According to the same rationale, if one singer can now be compared with other singers and his special qualities praised or disparaged, then each song (or each oral performance of a song) can be compared with others. For example, it now seems possible to speak of an "original" version of the song, different from other versions that are derived from it. If one of these songs is "true" because it has achieved a perfect fit of words to things, then any verbal difference between the true song and its derivatives will diminish truthfulness. Thus, his new verbal freedom brings the poet a dangerous responsibility. If he has begun by singing truly and strays progressively farther from his original performance, he may finish by singing "lies like true speech," a true song distorted by verbal variation with the passage of time. Song will change still more when it is transmitted from the first singer to a second, who must exercise his own verbal skill in performance, and so, although the singer's power to contrive allows Hesiod to establish himself as a unique authority, it also submits his work to the power of others.

Perhaps, then, the Muses' boast may be read as a commentary upon Hesiod's vulnerability. Since the Homeric bard does not control his language or compose his song, he need not concern himself with remembering precisely how the song first came to him; the song preserves itself under divine warranty, independently of tradition. Hesiod, on the other hand, evidently regards Memory as fundamental to his art, for he makes her the Muses' mother;[29] *alêthea*, the true speech opposed to the Muses' lies, may denote speech that is "unforgetting."[30] But with whose memory is he likely to be concerned? Hesiod does not seem to regard himself as indebted to other poets, and the Muses' honesty with him suggests that they will ensure the verity of his own performances. Thus, the poets who must remember are those who come after him, poets whose faulty recollection of Hesiod's authority may be represented by their dependence upon goddesses who lie.

Since the audiences of these poets will suffer the Muses' deceit, Hesiod also speaks to them. The audience seems helpless. As an activity of poets, true speech must arise from memory and false speech from forgetfulness. The audience, however, is made forgetful not only by deceit but also by song's truth, and so the audience cannot assume that it has been deceived whenever it becomes forgetful.[31]

Its helplessness also follows from the way one must now define likeness and difference in the expression *etumoisin homoia*. By taking *etuma* to mean "true statements" and as such the opposite of "lies" (*pseudea*), one denies them a common referent; lies must mimic truth only in form, from the listener's point of view. Once again, if this is what they say, the Muses tease men by insisting upon the esoteric nature of poetry; far from justifying Hesiod and themselves, they locate their art beyond public judgment, for they suggest that human audiences will never be able to distinguish or appreciate either their truthfulness or their deceptive skill.

The audience's inability to distinguish true and false statements does not, however, make them indistinct.[32] Hesiod evidently wishes to sing the truth (*etêtuma*, *WD* 10), not lies, and the fact that he must make such a claim for himself betrays his awareness of an alternative, even if audiences cannot immediately perceive it. It is now necessary to address the second question raised earlier in this chapter: what, if anything, makes the true song of the Muses different from the false for an audience? In particular, does the pleasure an audience may feel depend upon the singer's truthfulness? Hesiod's view of this problem can be inferred from the way in which he treats the psychology of pleasure in other contexts.

All song brings forgetfulness and memory, but true song brings its listeners forgetfulness of cares while it preserves their memory of the things it celebrates (*Th.* 53–55, 98–105). If false song produces a different and less happy effect, there must be another sort of forgetfulness that obscures the things song professes to describe but leaves undisturbed in memory the listener's cares. Lethe (*Lêthê*), the child of Strife (226–30), perfectly meets these requirements. Among her siblings are painful Toil (*alginoeis Ponos*), Hunger (*Limos*), Cares (*Algea*), Lies (*Pseudea*), and Doubtfulness (*Amphillogia*); as a family they are all set against the children of Pontos (233–36), particularly against Nereus, who is truthful (*apseudês*) and unforgetting (*alêthês*).[33] The baneful Lethe creates misery where true song relieves it, and works against our remembering the truth.

Hesiod does not expressly distinguish baneful from wholesome forgetfulness as effects of false and true song, but one finds them at work in two forms of a related art, the seductive speech of the king and the flattery of Pandora. The king is linked to poets by the Muse who attends him, Calliope "foremost of all" (*Th.* 79). He settles disputes with straight judgments (*itheiai dikai*, 86) and with rhetoric, "winning men over with gentle words" (90); his "words flow sweetly from his mouth" (84) like the poet's sweet voice described a few lines later (97). Since the king diverts men in assembly from their quarrels (86–90) as the poet makes his audience forget its cares (98–103), diversion (*parphasis*; cf. *paraiphamenoi*, 90) and forgetfulness are both beneficial here, alike opposed to baneful Forgetfulness, Strife's offspring and the sister of Cares (226f.).

But there is another sort of *parphasis*, corresponding to baneful Lethe, and it is described in quite different terms from the king's. Pandora, the woman fashioned of earth, is equipped with jewelry by Persuasion (*Peitho*, *WD* 73) and with false, flattering words by Hermes (*pseudea* and *haimulioi logoi*, 78). She seems to bring Epimetheus forgetfulness when she drives from his mind his brother's warning against the gifts of the gods, and when she opens her urn she "contrives grim cares" for men (85f., 95).

Pandora is a counterfeit fashioned in the likeness of a goddess (*WD* 62) or a respectable maid (71, *Th.* 572),[34] with evil intent. As a bane that looks "like" (*ikelos*) a blessing, she might be compared to false poetry that is "like" (*homoios*) true (*Th.* 27). According to this analogy, false poetry promises but withholds knowledge to men's sorrow; Pandora's beauty promises but destroys pleasure (cf. *WD* 57f.). For symmetry's sake, she should also foster ignorance, and she does so by denying men the blessings of divinity. Until her coming they have lived easily, without toil or disease (*WD* 90–92; cf. 109–13) and with untroubled hearts like the gods (112). Pandora helps Zeus to conceal this way of life (cf. *krupsantes . . . bion*, 42–49), revealing misery in its place.

As a poet inspired by the Muses (*Th.* 31), Hesiod reverses this process. He tells his listeners what the gods know, "the things that will be and those that were before" (32), especially the gods' own story (33), and he allows them, like the gods or men of the golden age, to free their hearts of care (97–99; cf. 61 and *WD* 112). Released from its present blighted condition, the audience of true song remembers for a moment an original knowledge and happiness, as men won over by the good king's *parphasis* forget their quarrels, and perhaps, like Nereus, remember instead "ordinances" (*themistes*, *Th.* 235; cf. *Il.* 1.238) that must come from Zeus (cf. *Od.* 16.403 and Zeus's "straight judgments," *WD* 36). The two sorts of forgetfulness and memory govern distinct categories of object. When they are beneficial, men forget their present trouble and remember distant truth, justice, and ease; when they are harmful, each takes the other's object, so that men forget the truth but learn misery. True and false words appear alike, as the Muses indicate, but as soon as one falls victim to deceit, one discovers the difference between them, as Epimetheus "knew his bane when he had it" (*hote dê kakon eikh' enoêsen*, *WD* 89).

Hesiod's audience therefore hears the same song Zeus hears, and, while it does, it shares the life of the gods it once possessed and lost. Zeus differs from men only because he suffers no present care, and so, since song merely confirms his memory of his own unflawed condition, he neither requires nor submits to forgetfulness.[35] For human beings, on the other hand, the truth of song brings happiness because it concerns something distant,[36] and to enjoy it they must take the risks that come from crossing a distance, relinquishing the present in forgetfulness. Although Hesiod cannot justify himself by an objective standard, because the past, the future, and the gods are always beyond human vision except in song, he seems confident that men will know from their own altered condition what sort of singer he is. For Hesiod, and then for Pindar, the psychology of the audience becomes a reliable index of the singer's truthfulness.

THE TECHNIQUE OF PIETY:

PINDAR

THE JUSTIFICATION OF HESIODIC POETRY IS BASED upon an implicit distinction and an implicit analogy. According to the first, the forgetfulness induced by song may be defined antithetically, by comparing it to another, harmful sort described by Hesiod, the forgetfulness induced by deceit; according to the second, the problem of judging the poet's art resembles the problem of judging the king's, for each art demonstrates its essential validity extrinsically, in the social benefits it confers. (Thus, the singer is truthful, and the king is just, when his words induce beneficent, pacific forgetfulness in his audience.) Pindar's account of his art makes both parts of this double premise explicit, elaborating the first into a systematic psychology of forgetfulness, a technical measure of the poet's success, and deriving from the second a doctrine of social poetics, which treats the poet as an active member of human society whose professional competence must be explained and judged in ethical terms.[1] For historical reasons, then, the technique of forgetfulness and the ethical basis of this technique emerge as major concerns in Pindaric poetics.

Hesiod's two categories of forgetfulness—beneficent and harmful—may be distinguished as Homer distinguishes two topics of song, the self and things outside the self: it is normally[2] desirable to forget one's own (especially painful) experience but undesirable to forget (or to be misled about) almost anything else. Pindar abandons the Homeric criterion and breaks down the Hesiodic categories by distinguishing with greater specificity the kinds of objects forgotten: when the elements of personal experience are variously assessed, for example, some may be judged worthy of recollection; conversely, it may be desirable to forget (or never to know) what others have done or endured. Thus, four categories of forgetting are created out of two (beneficent and harmful, of the self and of others), but there is no longer an easy way to distinguish beneficent forgetting from the harmful kind. In place of the Homeric rule (which requires that the singer pass over in silence his listener's personal concerns but commemorate the deeds of others with flawless integrity), Pindar offers complex, ethical justifications for his technique. The categories arrange themselves in pairs—the two ways of forgetting others, the two ways of forgetting oneself—and each pair is governed by its proper set of ethical standards, standards defined by piety.

In the eighth Nemean ode, Pindar defines the success of encomiastic poetry in terms of its treatment of Homeric topics, the deeds of heroes that must not be forgotten: the fate of Ajax, forgotten and obscure (24) despite his valor, indicates an absence and a misuse of the poet's arts; as a competent poet, Pindar offers his patron a better fate.

Odysseus is the poet's antitype: he misuses poetic technique, practicing "diversion" or "distortion" (*parphasis, N* 8.32) that makes Ajax obscure. In a benign form, this is the technique practiced with the Muses' help by Hesiod's king when he makes men forget their quarrels (*Th.* 80–93), but it resembles another, harmful *parphasis* worked by Calypso in the *Odyssey* and by Pandora in the *Works and Days* with seductive "wheedling" speech (*haimulioi logoi*).[3] Pindar reserves the term *parphasis* for harmful technique and elaborates its meaning so that it may serve to identify true song's chief antagonist:

> But see, there was, even in the past, hateful *parphasis*,
> companion of flattering (*haimuloi*) words,
>   contriving deceit, reproach that harms;

it does violence to the shining,
and offers up an unsound glory of unseen things.

(N 8.32–34b)

As a source of glory (*kudos*), *parphasis* mimics Pindar's art.[4] It works against the nature of its subject matter, however, making the "invisible"[5] somehow glorious and concealing manifest, shining things in obscurity. *Parphasis* is the art of slander (a deceitful kind of reproach) and flattery (a deceitful kind of praise), but Pindar's poetry praises only "things that deserve praising" and blames only the "wicked" (N 8.39). Apparently, the objects of praise and blame themselves dictate how the poet should approach them, and *parphasis* is harmful, by definition, because it violates this rule. Thus, true song seems less complicated and less meddlesome than deceit. Odysseus's lies resemble polychromatic, constantly changing patterns of light and darkness (cf. *aiolos*, 25), which add a superfluous intricacy to the things they illuminate.[6] Pindar stays on a "simple path" (35b–36). For this reason, *parphasis* is weaker than true song: when it flatters the "invisible," for example, it can produce only an attenuated, impermanent sort of glory, lacking substance like the invisible thing itself; sooner or later, the "invisible" naturally becomes invisible again, and Odysseus loses his false reputation for valor. The true praise Pindar offers—a boast that "fits" the thing (*prosphoron en . . . ergôi*, 49)—lasts like a stone (cf. P 3.114f.). In this way, then, Pindar distinguishes beneficent from harmful forgetfulness without having to specify which objects are best forgotten, for these things identify themselves by disappearing of their own accord.

It does not follow, however, that "shining" things (conversely) identify themselves unaided, without some added illumination,[7] and this asymmetry in the logic of *Nemea* 8 is the key to its rhetoric, which asserts the utility of Pindar's truthful epinician song and its obligation to offer praise.

Ajax shares with Odysseus the responsibility for his own dishonor, and he is drawn into a violent, ignominious conflict because he cannot speak for himself as Odysseus can do; his silence allows men to forget his valor (*N* 8.24), and so it permits Odysseus to fill an unnatural darkness with unnatural light. Ajax's fate indicates that the absence of song, of a proper defense against undeserved obscurity, can be as dangerous as *parphasis*, the misuse of poetic technique; silence as well as slander can be a kind of violence against nature. The epinician poet therefore must add some sort of verbal illumination to things in their natural state as a way of preserving nature. His role is active, and his contribution is substantial, necessary to the hero's "glory" (or the victor's) just as Odysseus's deceit is necessary to give the appearance of substance, by adding a false light, to things that have no substance in themselves.

If praise is useful because the poet adds something to the natural condition of what he memorializes, it is dangerous (*N* 8.20f.) for the same reason: there seems to be no absolute distinction between true poetry and *parphasis*, which also adds something to its objects (or, as slander, subtracts something from them). Encomiastic poetry, of course, can be justified, and its dangers made acceptable, in relative terms, for praise changes the condition of "shining" things less than silence would change it, and less than *parphasis* (flattery or slander) changes the condition of everything it touches.[8] There is a proportionality, a "fit" (48), between real achievement and valid praise. The validity of praise, however, is measured not simply as a function of accuracy; praise does not merely reflect its objects[9] (and some of Pindar's epinician poems scarcely mention the athletic victories they commemorate). Rather, the validity of praise is measured as a function of suitability.[10] Although Pindar's art is less complex than *parphasis*, it is not so simple as the truth.

The difference between suitability and truth becomes more explicit in *Nemea* 5:

> The exact truth is not all more profitable when
>   it shows its face;
> and silence is often the wisest thing for a man
>   to apprehend.   (16–18)

Silence of this kind must surely differ from the silence that ruins Ajax, the silence that works with *parphasis* to obscure shining things,[11] but it is the same in one respect at least: because it does not reveal the truth, Pindar's silence induces forgetfulness. There is, then, a desirable (useful and profitable) forgetfulness[12] like and unlike the undesirable kind, and its positive appeal must arise from suitability because it has nothing to do with the truth.

If silence can be suitable to its objects, then its objects must resemble "invisible things," for these are naturally forgotten and can only become known if speech does violence to nature. In *Nemea* 8, it seems, the "invisible" is something unreal, the valor Odysseus pretends to possess, but in *Nemea* 5 what the poet wishes to pass over in silence is something "great" (*mega*), a deed too large, rather than too small, for speech. In this case, apparently, the danger of speech (and so the need to keep silent) increases exactly in proportion to the deed's greatness. Thus, *mega eipein* (*N* 5.14) means "to speak of a great thing" and also, in normal usage, "to say something (excessively) great"; for Pindar, as for Homer, the quality of speech is given by the things one speaks about.[13] More specifically, a song about crime and danger becomes dangerous and criminal, for the "great thing" Pindar wishes to obscure is "a risk taken outside of justice" (14b), and its "greatness" is a measure of its criminality.

From the poet's point of view, therefore, a deed of criminal excess is the same as a deed not performed, an "invisible" thing such as Odysseus's achievement on the battlefield. The poet's silence, as the appropriate response to both extremes of enterprise, should make excess invisible, as "dark" as if it were nothing;[14] *parphasis* does the reverse, glorifying deeds not performed (as Odysseus glorifies his valor) and also glorifying crime. Thus, in *Nemea* 5, Hippolyta uses *parphasis* (32), "steep words" like the "great" words Pindar abjures, to make adultery an attractive prospect.

A moral principle apparently underlies the equation of criminal excess with inactivity, and this has yet to be explained, but its technical significance is more evident. In *Nemea* 5, silence occupies the position filled by reproach in *Nemea* 8, where Pindar presents himself as "praising what deserves praise and sowing blame among the wicked." As a response to crime, then, silence appears to be a kind of reproach, an active gesture of condemnation rather than simply the absence of speech; conversely, reproach, like silence, makes the criminal deed "dark,"[15] and so, in effect, it is the same as silence, something less than speech of the encomiastic, commemorative sort proper to song. As crime and inactivity are equivalent as topics of song, reproach and silence seem indistinguishable as technical instruments. Pindar's practice in *Nemea* 5 (14–18) reinforces this impression, for he explicitly condemns the deed he professes to obscure in silence. (This is a rhetorical trick, *paraleipsis*.) He dissociates himself from crime with an ambiguous, active sort of restraint, a half-spoken refusal to summon into view what should remain invisible.

It is now possible to array schematically one set of landmarks on the "simple path" of Pindaric technique, the rules for treating Homeric topics, "famous deeds" distant in time, performed by men other than the poet's audience. Homer regards none of these things as unsuited to song, for even the "hateful song" of Clytemnestra's crime must apparently last forever (*Od.* 24.192–202), but Pindar's task is different from Homer's, and so he makes distinctions where Homer does not. Because Pindar praises or blames (and does not merely commemorate), he apportions the facts into two categories, praiseworthy and unpraiseworthy; among things unworthy of praise, there are crimes,

deeds ambitious to excess, and also "invisible things" too
small to mention. For each topical category there is a single
Pindaric technique (praise for praiseworthy things, and reproach or silence, which are not clearly distinguished, for
everything else), and each technique works a single effect
(praise commemorates and reproach or silence obscures).
Parphasis, the antitype of Pindar's poetry, inverts the relationship between topic and technique, praising (and so
commemorating) things unworthy of praise but ignoring
or slandering (and so obscuring) things that "shine." The
principle underlying these rules (and the principle that
parphasis violates) is suitability: the poet must not speak too
much about crime nor say too little about virtuous achievement; his speech must be measured out in proportion to
the nature of its objects.

To apply this principle, however, the poet must know
what deserves praise and what does not; he needs a rule
for distinguishing crime from innocent, glorious achievement, and, if crime is an excessive deed (as *Nemea* 5 indicates), he needs a standard with which to define excess.
Again, the ideal is defined in terms of suitability and proportion, for every venture entails risk (cf. *O* 6.9–11, *O*
2.52) and so verges upon excess, just as there is always risk
in praising ambitions fulfilled (*N* 8.20f.). The second term
of the proportion, the standard against which excessive
criminal activity may be distinguished from *areta*, is the
god's plan for human fortune: what god (*P* 1.56f.) or Fate
(*N* 7.58f.) decides is, by definition, the "right amount"
(*kairos*) in every venture, and the poet may distinguish
praiseworthy and unpraiseworthy deeds on this basis. A
"thing without god," an act of excess, "is not worse for
being kept in silence" (*O* 9.103), but a man deserves praise
if his strength and success are "divine" (*daimonios*), god
given.[16] Thus, the poet apportions praise in the same way
that other men measure their efforts, according to god's
plan, which specifies the "right amount." Too much praise,
a boast, violates the *kairos* (*P* 10.4)[17] and, in the worst case,

poetic excess elevates men "out of proportion" (*para kairon*, *O* 9.35–39) by abusing the gods themselves. Pindar, on the other hand, accepts what the god gives (*P* 3.103f.) and subordinates his art to fortune (108f.)

Clearly, then, the *kairos* is "the best thing to know" (*O* 13.48), the best thing in poetic art because the *kairos* explains the rule of suitability, which takes precedence in various ways over the truth. According to one method of calculation, crime must be forgotten, like an "invisible" deed never in fact performed, because scant and excessive ventures are equidistant from the *kairos*, equally "without god"; and, if a crime by god's standard is no deed at all, commemorating the truth about such a thing must seem impious at best. (Thus, it is sometimes unprofitable to reveal "the exact truth," as this rule is formulated in *Nemea* 5.) However, according to another, more radical method of calculation, there can by definition be no impious truth because the "path of truth" is piety, acquiescence to god's plan, to the *kairos* (*P* 3.103); conversely, the *kairos* to which piety attends is, by definition, "truth" (cf. *N* 1.18b). God's standard, therefore, becomes the only standard, and there can be no truth about crime (as there is in *Nemea* 5) because crime, lacking god's endorsement, lacks reality. (Thus, if exceptions to the *kairos* are equivalent literally to nothing, the *kairos* is not merely the best but the only thing that can be known, and there is only one kind of knowledge, the knowledge of virtue.)

God's plan, however, is often obscure to human beings: "No clear sign (*tekmar*) from Zeus follows men" (*N* 11.44)[18] and "the streams of foresight are far away" (46). Even the poet exercises his technical skill always in some degree of uncertainty about god:[19] his hope for the future is in god's hands (*O* 13.103–5), and when he anticipates that a herald's true oath will confirm his praise (98–100), the truth of this imagined oath depends upon Zeus, "the one who accomplishes" (*telei'*, 115). Thus, Pindar resembles the hero Bellerophon, whose success remains "beyond oath of hope" (83). Because god's intentions can never be surely known, there seems to be no immediate remedy for the risks of praise. The "winged craft" of poetry (*potana makhana*) remains ambivalent, sometimes to be dreaded when it is devious like Homer's (*N* 7.22),[20] and some-times—as Pindar hopes, in his own case—a matter of pride (*P* 8.34f.)[21] when the poet's caution is rewarded and his thought coincides with divine purpose (cf. *P* 3.108f.).

Although the poet cannot perceive the *kairos* of praise-worthy deeds directly, he can detect god's presence and reduce the danger of speech in other ways. Ventures "without god" are undertaken by men who possess only "learned" or "acquired" abilities (*didaktai aretai, O* 9.100f.), men who have altered artificially their natural talents. As ventures "without god" are best kept in silence (*O* 9.103f.), men who use learning must remain incurably "obscure" (*N* 3.41); their achievements are not praiseworthy. The best foundation for success, on the other hand, and the source of abundant splendor, is what comes to men naturally, their congenital, inherited ability (*to de phuai kratiston hapan, O* 9.100; cf. *N* 3.40). God's supporting presence, it seems, expresses itself in "nature" (*phua*), and so Fate and "nature" become interchangeable terms (cf. *N* 7.54–58); each man's personal fortune—the decisive, divine factor in everything he does—is given to him at birth (*N* 5.40f.). This rule also applies directly to poets, for if their skills are ac-quired artificially, their efforts will be always excessive—an unrestrained, indiscriminate babble (*panglôssia, O* 2.86f.), out of proportion to the *kairos*—and always vain (*akranta, O* 2.87), without god-given strength. Thus, artificial skill resembles the *parphasis* of Odysseus, which adds an un-natural complexity to things but produces only weak "rot-ten" glory (*N* 8.34b): an artificial skill can produce nothing but artifice, unsuitable speech.

Because god's favor comes to men at birth, as an inher-ited product of their nature (*N* 3.40), it belongs to whole families, passing from one generation to the next in direct descent. In this way, god's favor follows a pattern—the "path" of nature is "straight" (*N* 1.25).[22] Since the man who wins false, impious success does not bequeath strength to his descendants, it is possible to assess the divine element in a deed of the past by examining the subsequent history of the hero's family. It is also possible to assess present deeds by examining the past: a man, more likely than not, acts in accordance with the *kairos* if his ancestors accomplished something notable, and he follows in their "tracks" (*P* 10.10–14, *N* 6.13–16).[23] Therefore, for the encomiastic poet who wishes to find the *kairos* for praise, the history of a family's achievement is decisive: an achievement that follows the pattern of race, that draws upon an inherited favor from god, can be praised safely because it reveals itself naturally.[24] As a topic for song, old inherited excellence justifies the poet's *makhana*, his ingenuity; it balances and controls what might otherwise become dangerous, that is, his ambition to say something that has never been said before. Thus, Pindar's claim that he follows a path marked out by earlier generations (*N* 6.53f.) supports his profession of originality:[25]

> Arouse for them a path of words clear-sounding;
> praise old wine, but the blossoms of song
> that are new.
> (O 9.47–49)

On this basis, the measure of what Pindar contributes to things by speaking about them, and men's need for his contribution, can be assessed again with greater precision. Although the path of "nature," of virtuous achievements endorsed by god, persists in a "straight" line through time from one generation to the next, the facts as men perceive them are less orderly. There are two versions of reality: one of them is divine, the sum of things within the *kairos* to which god gives strength and which can be described with the pious, selective sort of truth; the other is human, an amalgam of failure and success, crime and virtue, and here god's path may often seem obscure. Even for a family made

congenitally strong by god, success is at best intermittent,
and the family is like a field, at one moment bearing crops,
at the next lying fallow and gathering strength for another
season (N 6.8–11). During these fallow periods, according to another Pindaric image, in the intervals between
glorious achievements that shine with a "god-given splendor" (P 8.96f.), there is darkness: past splendor fades
unless singers praise it (N 7.12–16; cf. I 7.16–19). Thus,
although the virtues of heroes persist naturally in their descendants, unchanging nature may be hidden by changing
fortune. The illumination that encomiastic song adds to
the objects of praise, by leaping the intervals between success and connecting one moment of splendor to the next,
makes manifest the hidden foundation of present reality.
Song discovers god's order in the confusion of human experience, and so "makes the story straight" (O 7.21).[26]

The encomiast's ability to see through intervals of darkness, to perceive and to reproduce in song an orderly history of success, seems to be a fundamental element of his
art. He is perspicacious, wise (sophos)[27] about things hidden in time, in the same sense that time itself is "wise"
in separating the permanent from the ephemeral, real
achievement from appearances (O 1.33f.),[28] and he must
possess this capacity in greater measure than other men,[29]
or men would remember what the poet does not commemorate (cf. N 7.12f.). Men therefore require his services.
They depend upon the poet's special insight for immediate, practical reasons, for if they perceive and emulate
what their ancestors accomplished, their own present
"road" will be splendid (O 6.72) and they will abstain from
violence and crime (O 7.90–92). If they forget the past, on
the other hand, men also lose sight of what they must
presently do:

> . . . a cloud of forgetfulness comes confounding
> and wrenches the straight path of action
> from their minds.   (O 7.45–47)

Then, instead of proceeding in the "straight path" of their nature and god's plan, they are driven astray and deviate into excess (31).[30] To prevent such deviation, the poet displays praiseworthy deeds of the past as part of a pattern extending, ideally, through the present into the future (cf. *N* 1.25–28). His poem serves as an instrument of foresight by showing where fate or god has created an opportunity for virtuous successful endeavor, a *kairos*.

Eliding the darkness of crime and inactivity, encomiastic poetry evidently treats Homeric topics, the deeds of heroes, according to a rationale distinctly different from Homer's. At most, epic acknowledges its effect upon the "reputation" of the living: the "hateful song" of Clytemnestra blackens the name of virtuous women (*Od.* 24.200–202), but the women of posterity remain virtuous nonetheless and song never touches them directly. For Pindar, however, the past appears to be something always in essence present, because living men inherit divine favor from their heroic ancestors, and so the lessons of the past are also lessons for living men about themselves. The audience, then, may be regarded as a constant presence in encomiastic song, for Pindar concerns himself explicitly with his patron and his patron's fellow citizens whenever his attention shifts from the unchanging elements of their history. The result is a new intimacy between poet and audience and a new complexity in the poet's task: Pindar has insinuated himself, in the role of expert and teacher, between men and their own nature.

When the listener's direct personal interest in the topics of song is explicitly acknowledged, it lends a new aspect to the technical problem of matching speech to a *kairos* and of commemorating or obscuring things in a natural way. The *kairos* now appears to inhere not in things but in the listener's response to poetry: the poet will know that he has violated a subjective *kairos* when his poetry provokes anger or envy, for example (*P* 1.81–84).[31] Thus, to the calculus of

virtue and crime in the deeds of the past there is added a
calculus of feelings, of pleasure and pain in the audience.
In this light, the notion of a poetic technique in harmony
with nature must be reconsidered, for the natures of men
differ, and so the poet must discriminate among his listeners' innately dissimilar predilections as he discriminates
between the natural splendor and darkness of things. The
poet's technique, in either case, will remain nicely balanced
between adding nothing to nature and adding too much,
for in showing men themselves, Pindar aims at enhancing
his listeners' innate qualities rather than altering them, just
as he adds illumination only to things inherently splendid
and so supplements their natural memorability. Therefore,
he teaches men to "become, having seen" the sort of men
they are (P 2.72).[32] He acknowledges an absolute limit
upon his influence: men grasp his meaning only so far as
their nature allows (cf. O 2.83–86); and Pindar is a teacher
of virtue, but the virtue he teaches cannot be learned (cf. O
9.100–102).

The first Pythian ode addresses two corollary issues, as-
sessing the pleasant and painful effects of song upon various audiences and measuring the beneficent power of encomiastic technique against the natural tendencies of men
to forget or remember themselves.

Time is the active natural principle that governs memory
and forgetfulness. It is the cause of forgetfulness, and forgetfulness is the cause of memory:[33]

> I wish that all of time might . . . make him forget his
>   toils.
> So it would remind him in what battles of war
> he stood steady with enduring spirit.   (46–48)

Apparently, the pain concomitant with achievement suppresses the memory of achievement until time suppresses
the memory of pain, and so forgetting one aspect of experience is a precondition for remembering the other. Therefore, if a poet wishes to display before his listeners what

they have accomplished themselves, his poem must soothe them,[34] as time does, to make the demonstration painless; because it works more quickly than time, the poet's art enhances a natural tendency.

The extent to which poetry outstrips time gives the measure of its contribution to nature, to the evolution of painless self-awareness in the audience. The pain to be forgotten has a past and a future aspect: in the *Odyssey*, Odysseus weeps at Demodocus's song of Troy (8.83–95, 521–30) because he remains a wanderer, deprived of the gifts he won in battle; the memory of Troy shows Odysseus his persisting need to struggle, and his sense of having still to complete his story makes the early part of it too near to be contemplated with equanimity. Later, when he lies at home beside Penelope after he has killed the suitors and won his reward, there is no pain for him in recollection (23.200ff.). He has achieved the fixed state of Eumaeus, who remembers toils with pleasure (15.398f.) because he faces no repetition of the past and no future improvement of his lot.[35]

Pindar's poetry anticipates this fixed state so that it may do for Hieron what Demodocus's song could not do for Odysseus, make memory painless. The poet must abstract his listener as much as he can from the uncertainty of future toil, for painless memory requires "straight" (cf. *euthunoi*, P 1.46), unwavering possession of wealth;[36] since only time can bring this surely, the poet projects himself into the future to a point beyond vicissitude. As the steward of Hieron's reputation in song, he watches over a "boast to posterity" (*opithombroton aukhêma*, 92) that lasts forever (94), and he prays that Hieron may enjoy unchanging material fortune (46, 56f.).[37] Since his prayers are cast in the form of hypomnesis,[38] Pindar extracts assurance from the past; his method is circular, making past achievement serve as a sign of future happiness, which serves in turn to allow painless memory of achievement.[39]

Thus, Pindar's competence in reassuring his audience may be regarded as a function of *sophia*, his knowledge of

god's abiding presence in human history. Having discovered permanence in divine favor, however, Pindar's art obscures the temporality of fortunate historical events: the
poem equates the future with the past and offers its audience a timeless, abstracted perspective. If Hieron sees himself reflected in the unchanging medium of song, he will
learn to perceive both his past and his present from the
vantage of posterity, which does not distinguish between
them because it remembers both; since men remember
success but not pain, Hieron is taught by song to forget the
trouble he anticipates as well as the pain he once endured.

As a natural cause of selective forgetfulness, time offers
one model for Pindar's poetry; Apollo's lyre and the song
of the Muses offer another model,[40] a touchstone for distinguishing among the natures of audiences. Among the
gods, music subdues weapons, but it is a weapon itself; it
soothes the eagle of Zeus but terrifies his enemies. Half of
the lyre's effects are described in the manner of Homer and
Hesiod. The eagle is entranced or possessed (*kataskhomenos*, *P* 1.10) like Odysseus's listeners in Phaeacia (*Od.*
11.334); the gods are enchanted (*kai daimonôn thelgei phrenas*, *P* 1.12) by the lyre's shafts[41] like the Odyssean singer's
audience.[42] Even Ares is pleased by song (10–12), and the
lightning of Zeus is quenched (5f.). The gods seem to forget the struggles of war as Hesiod's audience forgets its
cares (*Th.* 98–103, 55) and as time will allow Hieron to forget his military toils.

On the other hand, since the Muses' song is also a war
cry (*boa*, *P* 1.13)[43] that terrifies the enemies of Zeus, it
seems to shatter the peace it imposed among the gods; it is
not simply narcotic, and its double capacity requires explanation. Pindar describes the terror of Zeus's enemies with
an epic word (*atuzontai*, 13) connoting the panic of soldiers
in disordered flight.[44] Panic is a kind of forgetfulness, forgetfulness of the practical means of saving oneself or of the
courage to do battle. In the *Iliad* the Achaeans flee in terror
(*atuzomenoi*, 18.7) when they have forgotten warlike joy

(*lêthonto de kharmês*, 17.759).[45] The helplessness of fright-
ened men is also a kind of enchantment: Poseidon charms
(*thelxas*) Alcathoos and stops him in his tracks to be killed
by Idomeneus (13.435); the enchanted man, like one terrified, forgets his courage (*toisi de thumon/ en stêthessin eth-
elxe, lathonto de thouridos alkês*, 15.321f.).

Thus, panic and sleep, the beneficent and harmful effects
of divine music in *Pythia* 1, are both forms of forgetfulness
or enchantment; the power of music is ambivalent, just
as Homeric enchantment and Hesiodic forgetfulness are
sometimes beneficent, sometimes harmful. According to
Homer and Hesiod, however, the effects of song are not
normally harmful, and so the enchantment worked by
song enjoys a privileged status: one assumes that it is different in essence from the harmful kind.[46] Pindar assimi-
lates harm as part of the Muses' art, but he makes up for
the loss of one distinction by introducing another. Although musical enchantment is now acknowledged to be
an ambivalent experience, the poet's audiences differ; one
sort of audience is privileged to win pleasure from enchantment, but musical terror strikes only wrongdoers,
the enemies of Zeus.[47] The sound that makes the gods
sleep is the same one that terrifies their enemies. It will
work the first effect because it works the second, and the
second because of the first, just as time preserves the memory of achievement because it dissolves recollection of pain
and obscures pain by awakening the memory of achievement. In each case, the effects of song arise automatically,
according to some natural principle upon which the poet's
art relies.

Independently, the two models for song in *Pythia*
1 account for three kinds of response: pleasant self-
forgetfulness (induced by time or divine music), painful
self-forgetfulness (induced by divine music), and pleasant
self-awareness (induced by time). Taken together, they imply the existence of a fourth response, painful self-
awareness, which Pindar invokes to explain the active vol-

cano Aetna, where a monster lies imprisoned. As the monster's roar may be harmoniously joined to the epinician song, painful self-awareness may be reconciled with the other effects of poetry.

Neither the gods nor their enemies forget themselves entirely. Like forgetfulness brought by time, the quiet imposed by Apollo's lyre and the panic inspired by the Muses' shout are incomplete. Thus, the fire of Zeus's thunderbolt remains eternal (*aeinaos*, *P* 1.6) even when quenched by song,[48] and Typho remains active, emitting fire from beneath the mountain despite his panic.[49] Fire and the crash of the erupting volcano (24, 26) are signs of his wakefulness, his awareness of his present condition, which must also entail memory of his defeat by Zeus. Hieron's defeated Tyrrhenian enemy also makes a sound, a lamentation brought on by the violence that destroyed his fleet (*nausistonon hubrin*, 72); may he be contained, Pindar prays, by this audible, remembered vision, immobilized and enchanted by painful self-consciousness.[50]

To account for these sounds as part of the epinician poem,[51] both of Pindar's models must be invoked. Like time, the monster's roar and the Tyrrhenians' lament induce memory and forgetfulness selectively; like divine music, the sounds selectively please and displease different audiences. Thus, the memory and forgetfulness induced are variously harmful and beneficent. For Typho and his violent human counterparts, the sound they make indicates an active memory of defeat and the continuing consciousness of pain; "possessed" by such cacophony, they forget their strength. Hieron, on the other hand, remains conscious of his strength, for the Tyrrhenians' lament preserves the memory of his victory and the volcano's roar commemorates the victory of Zeus. Hieron and his people can forget their pain, however, for the enemy's unquiet chagrin promises safety for the victors in the future.

Having undertaken to make men forget or remember themselves according to a variable standard that allows for

the differences between them, Pindar evidently acknowledges a new sort of responsibility for his audience. In Homeric terms, his task more closely resembles the public
speaker's than the singer's,[52] for the Homeric singer makes
no concessions to his listeners and so he practices his art
without concern for their moral qualities. As Phemius suggests, his truthful song pleases good and evil men alike,
and he sings in any case to a divine, unchanging audience
of Olympian gods.[53] The public speaker, on the other hand,
adapts his art to his listener's inclination because he speaks
not about some remote heroic venture but about his listener's present, personal concerns, and he speaks for the
sake of some immediate personal or social benefit. For example, he must keep silent, according to Pindar, if "sov-
ereign" speech becomes "battle's goad" (fr. 170 Bowra =
180 Sn-M).[54] Pindar represents himself as a member of society and his songs as the medium of a social relationship.
He professes to be inspired as an encomiast by personal
desire (N 4.35; cf. O 1.3f.), and he acknowledges a bond of
affection with his patron and his audience.[55] Like a marriage feast, the performance of an epinician poem celebrates a state of concord and of shared pleasure (O 7.1–12)
in which the city as a whole participates (cf. 93f.).[56] Because
the moral qualities of Pindar's listeners determine their
response to his poetry (so that true praise for virtuous
achievement will displease an evil audience), any conces-
sion that Pindar makes to please his listeners must be justified in moral terms. He may properly gratify only virtuous
inclinations, and for this reason (among others), he wishes
urgently to be associated only with virtuous men.[57]

Pindar's poetry may be compared, in this respect, to its
antitype *parphasis*, which perverts healthy social relationships. When Odysseus slanders Ajax in the eighth Nemean ode, the Danaans respond with "service" that flatters Odysseus (*therapeusan*, 26): one form of *parphasis* seems
to inspire another[58] in reciprocation, so that the false encomiast and his audience are somehow mutually deceived

and mutually corrupted. The quality of their "secret" [59] political accommodation becomes apparent in its result, for it
provokes a "grim quarrel" with the slighted hero Ajax, and
the bloodshed that follows spoils his honor as if *parphasis*
had corrupted even its innocent victim. [60]

The violence that attends cooperation among false, de-
based men reflects the influence of Aphrodite's herald, [61]
who touches some not with gentle hands but "with another sort" (*heteron d'heterais*, N 8.3). Thus, *parphasis*, conventionally conceived as seduction, [62] becomes one of two
sorts of "erotic" social behavior. Aphrodite's benign influence, and a better sort of social temper, surrounds the king
"best in deeds of hand and in counsels," ever in men's regard, whom heroes obey unbidden (7–10): in the king's relationship with his subjects and neighbors, a relationship
inspired by one of the "nobler desires" (*tôn areionôn erôtôn*,
5), love's "gentle hands of necessity" (3) evoke willing obedience (9f.). This is the peaceful, constructive sort of accommodation Pindar's poetry seeks to produce. [63] While the
false, seductive power of *parphasis* brings death to Ajax and
"rotten" glory to his enemies, the pleasures distributed by
Pindar (38, 43f.) seem to engender excellence, which grows
like a vine, a product of noble *erôs*, among wise and just
men (41). [64]

The rationale for Pindar's distribution of pleasure, and
so of pleasing self-forgetfulness as it is described in *Pythia*
1, may therefore be sought in this notion of *erôs* as a social
force that draws men together in pursuit of excellence or
drives them apart in pursuit of less wholesome objects.
The "nobler" *erôs* fulfills itself by observing a *kairos*, a
"right amount" of desire (N 8.4f.), [65] and so Pindar distinguishes the different sorts of appetitive feeling that determine his listener's response to poetry as he distinguishes
historical facts that his poetry commemorates, according to
a rule of proportion. In each case, Pindar attempts to narrow the focus of his art. His "straight" narrative of the past
is strictly edited so that deviations from the *kairos* may be

made to fall out of account; the result is a rectified, simplified image of historical reality, in which failure and crime
remain invisible. The contemporary social context of his
poetry, the disposition of his audience, presents a similar
problem, for Pindar is obliged to walk upon "crooked
paths" when he confronts his enemies (*P* 2.84f.), deceitful
men inclined toward complexity (cf. 82), yet his own emotional inclination is "straight" (*eutheia tolma*, *O* 13.12).[66] His
straight feeling induces him to maintain a single, simple
standard of "straight" speech as he practices his art in
varying political circumstances (cf. *P* 2.86). He invokes the
kairos as a way to distinguish, and in some manner to discount, the excessive, "deviant" *erôs* that confuses this ideal
simplicity. The result is a selective, edited inventory of the
wholesome social feelings to which Pindaric poetry properly adapts itself.

Like the *kairos* of truth, the *kairos* of desire is defined by
god. One desires the right amount when one desires what
god is willing to give, a "measured quantity" of profit (*metron*).[67] A larger *erôs* is "madness" (*mania*), for it is predi-
cated upon an expectation (*elpis*) of success that, lacking
god's endorsement, must be deluded, "empty," and vain
(*N* 11.45–48; cf. *N* 8.45). This is Ixion's malady: he wants
more than his god-given privilege, and so, ignoring the
metron, he becomes crazed with a passion for Zeus's wife
(*mainomenais phrasin . . . erassato*, *P* 2.25–30; cf. 34); his unmeasured *erôs* may be regarded as an exemplary case of
impiety. Because the impious man's *erôs* can never be sated,
it seems to express itself naturally as an "envious," "nig-
gardly" disposition (*phthonos*) toward other men. Thus, his
ever-frustrated, ever-renewed hopes may be called "envious" (*phthonerai . . . elpides*, *I* 2.43): envy and hope arise
from the same "empty" vanity, a willful misapprehension
of god's inexorable purpose (*N* 4.39–41, fr. 200 Bowra =
212 Sn-M).

Since hope and envy are alike, it makes sense that a
single countervailing quality cures both. The hope that in-

duces unmeasured desire is "unrestrained," "shameless"
(*anaidês elpis*, N 11.45–48)—it lacks *aidôs*. *Aidôs*, then, tem-
pers desire and so induces a man to accept however much
or little god properly allows him.[68] And if, having accepted
his own fate, he accepts without *phthonos* the good fortune
of others, he feels another, related sort of *aidôs*, "regard" or
"reverence" for god-given excellence.[69] Both sorts of *aidôs*
are based upon piety:[70] the first is applied by each man to
his own case, to reconcile *erôs* with its fated satisfaction,
and the second is expressed socially, to reconcile men of
different fortunes. According to this scheme, one may deduce the influence of *aidôs* upon the heroes who, attending
to a *kairos* of *erôs*, willingly obey their splendid king in
Nemea 8.[71]

Phthonos and *aidôs*, then, are social symptoms of the different kinds of *erôs*, and they are associated typically with
different kinds of encomiastic behavior, which *erôs* also
controls. Because an envious man desires for himself what
he might have admired in others (cf. N 3.29f.),[72] he withholds the praise that excellence deserves (I 1.43–46, O
6.74–76); by denigrating god-given success (and therefore
denigrating the gods themselves),[73] he denies his own in-
feriority. Thus, in violating a *kairos* of feeling, an envious
encomiast also violates the rule of suitability in praise (I
5.24), and this means that he practices *parphasis*, like Odysseus in *Nemea* 8. An envious audience responds in kind: it
will be pleased by the fictions that *parphasis* contrives because it is displeased by the facts of divine dispensation (P
2.88–90, N 8.21). Envy (N 8.21) inspires the Danaans' secret assent to Odysseus's seduction, for example, and a
similar disposition, unmeasured *erôs*, accounts for Ixion's
delight in "sweet fiction" (*pseudos gluku*, P 2.37), the empty
pleasure he obtains from the cloud that Zeus has fashioned
in the image of Hera.

Pindar's encomiastic behavior, on the other hand, is governed by *aidôs*, which inhibits him from practicing *parphasis*[74] and makes him fit to offer praise. With a moderate

sort of *erôs*, seeking no more satisfaction than the present allows, he regards his friend's success as a favor to himself because it offers him an opportunity to exercise his encomiastic skill (*P* 10.64–66).[75] Evidently, Pindar feels no *phthonos*, and so he finds it easy to honor another man's excellence (*I* 1.43–46; cf. *N* 3.29). Thus, he demonstrates that he is a "wise man" or a "competent poet" (*anêr sophos*, *I* 1.45), and his competence consists not only in technique or in knowledge (the ability to perceive what deserves praise and what does not) but also in disposition, his ungrudging readiness to acknowledge what he knows.

Ideally, by distributing praise where it is deserved, Pindar's poetry also enhances his listeners' disposition to feel *aidôs*, "regard" for the achievement of an athlete victorious in the games.[76] His ability to work such an effect is limited, however, for some members of his audience will inevitably feel *phthonos*,[77] and Pindar's willingness to accept this limitation indicates that he regards immoderate *erôs*, the cause of *phthonos*, as an immutable fact of human nature, which he can no more change than he can change the facts of history. Therefore, Pindar's song will evoke the "regard" of *aidôs* only in men who feel the "restraint" of *aidôs*; as innate tendencies, *erôs*, *aidôs*, and *phthonos* resist artful manipulation.

Within the restricted circle of men whose desires are naturally restrained, encomiastic song exerts its wholesome social influence by offering moderate satisfactions, by enlarging the pleasure of one man's athletic victory so that his fellow citizens may share it, for example (*O* 7.93f.). Moderate satisfactions apparently reinforce moderation, for they soften the discomfort of unfulfilled ambition that even virtuous men experience in the course of changing fortune. Thus, the "charm" of song (*philtron*, *P* 3.63–65; *epaoidai*, *N* 8.49) is also an instrument of orderly restraint (*metron*);[78] the forgetful, enchanted ease that music evokes (*P* 1.1–12) may be identified with the "fair-sounding" celebrations enjoyed by cities (38), and both in turn with "harmony,"[79] the peaceful condition of men who agree to pay their fellows honor (70).[80]

As Pindar represents his art, his technical skill consists chiefly in discrimination and his spiritual competence in restraint. Among the facts of history he distinguishes brilliant, enduring achievements from empty perversions of fate, just as he distinguishes, among rhetorical practices, the proper means of pleasing a virtuous audience from illicit appeals to immoderate temperaments. Since the facts of history follow an unchanging pattern of divine influence that unites the past with the present, ancient deeds of valor with contemporary athletic victories, every topic of encomiastic poetry touches its audience directly, and the tasks of history and rhetoric coincide. Both are governed by a rule of piety, a constantly renewed calculation of god's benign presence, and the poet's success in making this calculation depends upon *aidôs*, his restrained, reverent disposition. *Parphasis*, poetry's antitype, discards the inhibition of *aidôs*, and so it falsifies the calculation required by piety, "distorting" the facts and "misdirecting" human feeling.

Pindar practices his art within the limits imposed by *aidôs* because, like any other human being, he can never be certain of success. His perspicacity, like all distinctive human abilities, comes from nature and from god,[81] but, like all divine gifts handed down to men from a source they cannot observe directly, it does not submit to exact measurement. In principle, there are limits to *sophia* that cannot be known in advance[82] because the gods allow men only partial knowledge of their plans,[83] and so, even as a "wise man," the poet remains vulnerable to error (*hai de phrenôn tarakhai/pareplangxan kai sophon, O* 7.30f.).[84] Thus, sober piety rather than inspiration or passion guides Pindar to the truth (cf. *O* 1.35). He does not enjoy Hesiod's intimacy with the Muses,[85] and he does not receive his verses ready-made from god, like a Homeric singer; *mania*, which Plato regards as the poet's source of insight, seems impious and destructive to Pindar.[86] His own measure of self-confidence (*tolma*, *O* 13.11f.; cf. *O* 9.80–84) is by contrast chastened, made "straight" and safe by piety. The impression of an inspired disorder in Pindar's poetry seems false in this light: he writes, by his own account, according to a *kairos* that has been carefully calculated and piously observed. If the "straight" path of his narrative seems arbitrary to his audience, this shows only that he knows better than his audience what the gods allow, not that he has achieved his special insight through some impenetrable, irrational process.

Pindar's ambivalent, cautious confidence reflects, perhaps, an unresolved doubleness in his account of what the poet does. As a master of speech, for example, he is *heurêsiepês* (*O* 9.80), one who "invents" or else merely "finds" the words of poetry. As an "invented" thing, Pindar's poetry is a product of human skill; as a "found" thing, it is divine.[87] Coincidentally, as an instrument for the preservation of truth, the encomium variously preserves a human and a divine sort of truthfulness. According to god's standard, crime and failure lack reality; they are by nature "dark," and so they can be truthfully obscured by the poet's silence. For human beings, on the other hand, crime and failure are real, and so, according to human standards, it is not truthful (although it is "suitable") to obscure these things. To the extent that they are real, crime and failure require an active response from the poet, something more than silence: Pindar reproaches criminal behavior, and so he seems to commemorate it. Thus, while his silence about crime may be regarded as a truthful reflection of divine reality, his reproachful speech evokes a view of reality that belongs specifically to human beings. As silence and reproach merge in Pindaric technique, the two views of reality merge also, and Pindar's program becomes equivocal.

By suppressing the memory of crime and failure (historical events that indicate an absence of god's favor) and by "turning the fine things outward" (P 3.83), Pindar professes to construct an edited, partial representation of human experience in which only "shining" achievements remain visible. As he has endowed impersonal epic topics (the "famous deeds of men") with personal relevance for his audience, he has, conversely, made the affective mechanisms of epic (enchantment and "forgetfulness of cares") into principles of historical knowledge: the encomiast's audience forgets not only its own trouble but also dark and threatening episodes of the past. The motive for Pindar's apparently exclusive attention to triumphant virtue is *aidôs*, pious caution, but caution marks its way by negative, monitory signs, and so it presupposes some persistent awareness of human vanity, a lingering memory of failure and vice.[88] "Turning the fine things outward" (P 3.83), then, accounts for only a part of the knowledge that Pindar values. The other part, the inward-turning, private knowledge of the dark intervals that separate moments of brilliance, lies concealed[89] behind the encomiast's celebration of *areta*, although it emerges occasionally, half-acknowledged, in the ambiguous form of half-silent reproach. Thus, Pindar's art stops short of tragedy. Because the encomiastic program cannot wholly assimilate mixed human experience, it cannot justify itself unequivocally. It remains poised between silence and speech, in obedience to Pindar's divided caution and confidence.

CHAPTER FOUR

MAGICAL FIGURES: AESCHYLUS
AND THE MEANING OF STYLE

SIMPLE SPEECH CONVENTIONALLY INDICATES A truthful speaker;[1] according to Pindar, contrived, "complicated" (*poikilos*) stories are false.[2] But there must also be another sort of complexity that does not diminish the truthfulness of speech, for the verbal style and the narrative structure of Pindar's own poetry are surely not plain, and Pindar's complexity[3] may be plausibly regarded as an honest virtue: his narrative mimics the timeless connectedness of the gods' dispensations of grace, and his style is the product of an instinctual art,[4] directed toward an audience instinctively perceptive of its meaning, of its "arrows speaking to the wise."[5]

The notion of a valid complexity will be the topic of this chapter, specifically, the notion of poetic truth that underlies Aeschylus's uniquely dense figurative language in the *Oresteia*. Aeschylus's language requires examination for two reasons: he seems to be self-conscious about using complex devices of style; he presents his language as a thing of guaranteed validity, valid when it is least intelligible and valid when it is clear.

Metaphors and oxymora, the most striking Aeschylean figures, do not occur randomly throughout the trilogy; they are clustered at its start, in the *Agamemnon*, and in succeeding plays their frequency declines.[6] Aeschylus, evidently, knows more than one style, and his stylistic decisions must be deliberate because his dramatic characters speak about style explicitly. The chorus, for example, remarks upon the absence of imagery (*exêikasmena*)[7] in Cassandra's oracles: when she has begun to express herself literally (*Ag.* 1178–83), her speech no longer seems vague; it simply denotes one thing, to which the chorus can put a name (Thyestes, 1242).

The dramatic characters' choice of style is made meaningful by a necessary, magical connection between words and the things they signify, and this is the second reason why the complexity of Aeschylean language needs (and allows) examination. Even without the speaker's knowledge, language automatically reflects the nature of the world: meaning inheres in the syllable, in the sound of words, so that words that sound alike mean similar things. Applied to Aeschylus's numerous etymologies,[8] this principle suggests the near-equivalence of Fury (*Erinys*) and strife (*eris*), War (*Arês*) and curses (*arai*), Zeus and his daughter Justice (*Dikê, Dios korê*); and it suggests an unbroken continuity when Phoebus receives his name and Delphi from Phoebe at the same time (*onoma . . . parônumon, Eu.* 7f.). More problematically, Helen has been "truly" and "appropriately" named (*etêtumôs, Ag.* 682; *prepontôs,* 687) because her fate has been destructive, confirming the sense of the syllable *hel-*. Yet the revelation of her name's truth comes to the chorus only after the fact, as a divine contrivance understood with difficulty: throughout her life, Helen has been correctly addressed as "destroyer" by speakers who were ignorant of the significance of their speech. The truth of speech seems alien to the speaker in a different way when the chorus listens unwillingly to the song of vengeance and disaster that its own heart sings, at once "self-taught" (*autodidaktos, Ag.* 992), like Phemius in the *Odyssey* (22.347f.), and inspired by a Fury, as Phemius is inspired by the god. This song that virtually sings itself[9] is guaranteed to be true because the words are not chosen but come ready-made with the facts; the chorus prays that it may be false, but vainly (998–1000).[10]

The magical validity of words also operates actively, by influencing the nature of things. Thus, although men sometimes fail to control their speech or to grasp its significance, it changes the world around them. The *klêdôn* is a word or expression that validates itself magically,[11] and prayers are sometimes formulated on this basis, calling upon the god to fulfill the promise signified by his title: thus, in *Seven against Thebes* (9), Eteocles asks that Zeus defend men "true to his name" (*epônumos Alexêtêrios*), and Orestes summons Hermes to be a guide "true to his name" (*epônumos pompaios*) in the *Eumenides* (90f.) (cf. *Ag.* 973f.). Evil too may be summoned by the word that describes it: when Cassandra tells the chorus bluntly of Agamemnon's death, the chorus demands silence (*euphêmon stoma, Ag.* 1247);[12] if evil is desired, on the other hand, the evil word once spoken is accepted, as the chorus "accepts" Aegisthus's death when he names it (*Ag.* 1653).[13]

Because language magically reflects and influences the world, the spoken word poses a problem of knowledge and power for each of the dramatic characters. The words each one hears must be thoroughly understood as an index of wanted and unwanted truth, with uncounted implicit meanings potentially contrary to what the speaker wishes to communicate. The words each one utters must also be understood, so that their implicit sense may be controlled and directed toward some desired reality, as Clytemnestra implicitly conjures into being what she pretends to deprecate when she describes the Achaean army's impiety and Agamemnon's death.[14] Thus, Aeschylus's equivocal language becomes the dramatic character's predicament. One aspect of this predicament, the problem of knowledge, seems pertinent also to his audience, for the audience must evidently understand the play's equivocality better than any dramatic character. Therefore, perhaps, the *Oresteia* invites the audience to build its interpretive method upon the magical validity language enjoys within the dramatic fiction; proceeding from that premise, one may expect to discover something about the meaning of Aeschylean complexity and, incidentally, to discover why metaphors and oxymora are more numerous in the *Aga-memnon* than elsewhere.

Oxymora typify a more extensive class of linguistic phe-nomena, the class of words or phrases that seem to con-tradict themselves. Oxymora denote a union of two things that do not, according to common or conventional sense, belong together, and the strongest are those that violate lexical definitions: in the expression "graceless grace" (*akharis kharis*, *Ag*. 1545; cf. *Ch*. 42 emend. Elmsley), the second word seems to cancel the first (or the first the sec-ond), for the thing so named is said both to be and not to be *kharis*; the "tuneless tune" (*nomos anomos*, *Ag*. 1142; cf. 1473) is a melody that renders meaningless the notion of melody because it is and is not "tuneful." [15] The negative term is formed on the same root as the positive one and is therefore (as long as the root bears the same meaning in both its forms) [16] its opposite. At the same time, however, the magical principle that similar sounds denote similar things, or things harmoniously combined, suggests that the positive and negative terms may be tied to one another more closely. *Kharis* and *akharis*, for example, sound as nearly alike as Phoebus and Phoebe, and the similarity of sound insists upon their identity, which the lexical mean-ing of the words denies. The most compact and radical phenomenon of this kind is a single word denoting two opposed things because the sounds associated with each thing are not merely similar but the same. Thus, the word *kêdos* (*Ag*. 699), which identifies Helen as both a "relative by marriage" and a "source of woe" for the Trojans, indi-cates phonetically some sort of necessary or natural unity among things that do not belong together.

Some of the issues at stake in this conflict between sound and expected sense have been historically defined for Aeschylus by Hesiod and Heraclitus. [17] For chiefly ethi-cal reasons, Hesiod argues strenuously against the identity of zealous competition and vicious contention, two sorts of strife named by the single word *eris* (*WD* 11–26). If the equivocality of the word reflects an inevitable confusion among the things named, human beings will be unable in practice to behave with healthy zeal, or with simple justice, in a manner pleasing to Zeus.[18] Or, if the two sorts of strife essentially differ (and if just behavior cannot be unjust), equivocality will falsify the language of the poet who attempts to teach simple justice, for *Amphillogiai* (ambiguities, disagreements) are the sisters of Lies (*Th* 226–30). For the sake of justice and the knowledge of justice, therefore, Hesiod self-consciously undertakes a correction of language. He sacrifices another sort of certainty, however, because language that can be manipulated in this way ceases to be what Homer would call "self-taught." (The Homeric poet is "self-taught" because he learns the words of his song not from other poets but from the facts themselves, as if the facts dictated the language that must be used to describe them; thus, it seems that Homeric song can never be false. For Hesiod, on the other hand, there seems to be no guaranteed correspondence between facts and the language of poetry: if his language must be manipulated, it can be manipulated wrongly.) This is the danger represented by the Muses, who "know how to make many false statements that are like true ones" (*Th.* 27). *Amphillogiai*, then, have not been eliminated; rather, one uncertainty (about the truthfulness of song) has replaced another (about song's meaning). Given the equivocality of words like *eris*, Hesiod has been forced to choose between the certain knowledge of justice and the guaranteed truth of poetry.[19]

Heraclitus seems to accept the conflict of sound and conventional sense as a fact of nature: as if to challenge the case for simplicity, he remarks (fr. 48) that the name of the bow (*bios*, accented on the second syllable) is "life" (*bios*, accented on the first syllable), but its effect (*ergon*) is death; since life and death are "the same" in his view (*tauto*, fr. 88), he evidently wishes to show that the sound of the bow's name correctly identifies its deadly effect with life and that the complexity in the relationship between words and things speaks more truly than human speakers know.[20] Therefore, Heraclitus must confront more directly the problem Hesiod wishes to eliminate, the need to elicit from equivocal language its proper, and unsuspected, complex significance. In this respect, oracular speech seems to be the type of all true speech for Heraclitus:[21] it neither "speaks" (*legei*) nor "conceals" (*kruptei*) but rather "indicates" (*sêmainei*).[22] The truth contained in oracles, and in all speech, remains superficially unintelligible because oracles do not "speak" or explain themselves, but the truth is also not "concealed" because, if words and things are naturally related, the unintelligibility of speech corresponds to a similar quality in things, indicating, on the analogy of its own structure of sound and sense, a "hidden harmony" that is necessarily hidden, as the tension in a bowstring is invisible.[23] Thus, Heraclitus chooses between falsely simplified language and language neither more nor less clear than what it describes.

The simplification disallowed by Heraclitus's oracular speech, and by Aeschylus's oxymoronic figures, works chiefly by eliminating unwanted meaning: thus, Hesiod discounts "contentiousness" as the meaning of *eris* when he wishes to denote "zeal." The translation of figurative into literal language, which also works by eliminating meaning, must also be disallowed, and so, in magical language, the distinction between figurative and literal has no significance. One sees a figure in Aeschylus's phrase "graceless grace," for example, on the assumption that grace cannot be literally "graceless," and one interprets the figure by specifying in what way it makes literal sense, in what way not. An action may be regarded as a pleasing favor by one participant, as a painful injury by another; it may be formally gracious but essentially hostile because it fulfills an empty, onerous obligation; and it may be meant as a fine thing although really and unintentionally an ugly one. In any of these ways of reading (and all of them more or less suit the context of *akharis kharis* at *Agamemnon* 1545), translating the figure into a literal statement entails a selective and ethical judgment on the reader's part, a judgment that assigns weight to one participant's pleasure rather than another's, to the essential rather than the formal sense of the action (or the reverse), or to the intentional rather than the unintentional sense (or the reverse). Then one can say that the "graceless grace" is not a grace at all, or else that it is not graceless, and the figure generated by the juxtaposition of the two words will be made literal when one of them is eliminated.[24] It is tempting to suppose that this is what Heraclitus ridicules in fragment 87 ("a stupid man tends to flutter at every word"): if words are treated as the basic units of meaning, the figurative sense generated by phrases will be lost.[25]

In its proper, unsimplified form, the figure *kharis akharis* impartially connotes the complete, unconventional array of its single, more conventional meanings, for if verbal complexity corresponds naturally to real complexity, a partial reading violates the figure's nature. The same principle that forbids eliminating from the phrase one of two contradictory words also forbids eliminating one meaning from the several belonging to a single word. *Nomos*, then, means not only "tune" or "law" but both of these things. Finally, when polysemous words in combination generate figurative meaning, a corollary principle forbids transforming the figure into a literal statement by limiting the sense of any single word. Therefore, the figure *nomos anomos* (*Ag.* 1142), which means "lawless tune" (an easy, literal reading), connotes with equal validity "lawless law" (an oxymoron), "tuneless tune" (another oxymoron), and "tuneless law" (a metaphor).[26] Ideally, it seems, complex magical language requires exhaustive interpretation, but perhaps interpretation is best characterized negatively, as an undiscriminating, passive sensitivity to meaning that should properly come, automatically and unbidden, with the sound of speech.[27] Thus, it will be relatively easy to apprehend the complex sense of *nomos anomos* if one refrains from interpreting the phrase according to some limited, personal notion of what makes probable or acceptable "sense."[28]

The problematic of interpretation, which seems to vanish (or else to grow beyond management) in this account of magical speech, emerges again in another form, as the problematic of necessity and choice: understanding and accepting the sense of figures that represent naturally complex things become matters of understanding the necessity that generates complexity in the world. Thus, in an expression describing Agamemnon (*Ag.* 224f.), the sounds of *thutêr* ("sacrificer") and *thugatros* ("of his daughter") indicate that the two words are somehow predisposed to combination, that some natural tendency underlies Agamemnon's offense against nature; and this predisposition embodied in the sound of words is perhaps the "yoke of necessity" (218) to which Agamemnon submits when he performs the sacrifice.[29]

The necessity from which such complexity arises seems to operate at three levels, first and most patently as the circumstantial context that endows chosen action with unwanted significance. For example, in the "graceless grace" of Clytemnestra's funeral rite for Agamemnon, there is a conflict between her duty as a wife, which is fixed by circumstance, and her behavior as a killer, which Clytemnestra chooses freely, apparently with pleasure; violating her marital duty makes Clytemnestra's behavior complicated and criminal, and so she denies her identity as Agamemnon's wife (cf. *Ag.* 1498f.);[30] complexity is necessary only in the sense that circumstance (half of the oxymoron) cannot be validly omitted from "interpretation."

But clearly, if Clytemnestra were not Agamemnon's wife, she would not choose to kill him; her chosen behavior is based upon something complex and unalterable in the past, the sacrifice of Iphigenia, which belongs in turn to a pattern of disturbed relationships among members of the Atreid family. Thus, the family's little universe is ruled by a law of contradiction, so that alienation and violence inevitably accompany intimacy and love, and the Atreids' natural tendency toward complexity determines their choices. Therefore, the complex sense of language—notably, the complex sense of *kêdos* ("relation by marriage" and "source of woe")—is not partly necessary and partly chosen, although it is often only partly acknowledged. Rather, the family's nature generates oxymoronic description as it generates crime, and the origin of this rule may be traced back to the first of the family's crimes. When Atreus serves Thyestes his children's flesh for dinner, he destroys, apparently forever, the possibility of simple definitions: the children's identity is so overloaded with significance in this perversion of human custom that they become "unidentifiable" or "unmeaningful" (*asêma, Ag.* 1596).

Finally, the little Atreid universe ruled by contradiction proves to be a model for something larger. This is the lesson of the Trojan war, which suffers inherently from the same unwanted significance that complicates intimate Atreid behavior: Thyestes' curse does not so much contaminate the war as the war provides a new source of power for Thyestes' curse. In the portent that prefigures Troy's destruction, twin eagles devour a pregnant hare (*Ag.* 115–20), and its pregnancy makes excess unavoidable, for they cannot kill the hare without also killing its (innocent) children. Thus, the war, an enterprise undertaken to vindicate Zeus's justice, is also unjust; it is necessarily in contradiction with itself and "pregnant" with meaning. Agamemnon actively accepts the portent in its undiminished sense when he agrees to Iphigenia's sacrifice, another complex "sign" of the war's nature.[31] The complexity he accepts, however, comes first of all, ready-made, from the gods. Iphigenia's death offends the deity whose demand[32] it gratifies; Zeus's justice contaminates its agents. Apparently, there is a divine contradiction that resembles and reinforces the Atreids' ingrown tendency toward crime.

The figure *thutêr thugatros*, then, indicates three kinds of necessity in the sacrifice of Iphigenia: the natural fact of kinship, violated by Agamemnon's choice; the Atreids' incurable, congenital pollution; and Zeus's justice, of which the sacrifice is a "sign."

The gods' complexity, like Atreid crime, generates oxymoronic description, dangerous speech, which human interpreters anxiously and vainly attempt to simplify. Cassandra's hopeless, inspired oracles typify the danger, an inauspicious "dysphemism" (*dusphêmousa, Ag.* 1078) that confounds unequivocal definitions of the gods. Apollo's nature, she suggests, is magically revealed by the sound of his name, "destroyer" (*apollôn* as if *apalluôn*, 1081). Since Apollo is also the god of healing (cf. 146, 512f.) invoked to celebrate occasions of victory and joy, celebration will be always tainted by his name's unwanted darker significance, a fact reflected in human experience by the affinity between health and disease (cf. 1001–4).[33] The herald's cautious "euphemism" (636), on the other hand, typifies speech artificially simplified in accordance with a more hopeful theology: he clings to the notion that reporting bad news on a happy occasion is a kind of impiety because the gods of suffering are properly kept distinct from the gods of good fortune, the Furies from the Olympian gods (636–49).[34] The chorus professes a form of piety uncertainly located between the herald's euphemism and Cassandra's dysphemism, hopeful or hopeless depending upon circumstances: at first its prayers celebrate the power of a god whose name it does not surely know (160–66);[35] later it discovers the god's identity in the name "Zeus" (1485f.), but the name cannot be reduced to a simple definition, for it signifies the cause (in the sounds *Dios*, "of Zeus," and *dia*, "on account of") of everything that happens. Good and evil on a cosmic scale are inseparably joined in the single word, an implicit source of uncounted oxymora.

Metaphors, like oxymora,[36] are portentous in the *Oresteia*, a magically valid index of complexity in the actions of men and the nature of gods, but their validity is perhaps more evident, and their complexity is certainly greater. As valid omens, the figures "materialize,"[37] become visible and effective: when Agamemnon describes the Argive "host" (*leôs*, *Ag.* 825) as a "lion" (*leôn*, 827), the figure's sound suggests a natural affinity between man and beast (*dakos*, 824); Clytemnestra sees this affinity, which is normally hidden,[38] when she dreams of Orestes as a snake (*dakos*, *Ch.* 530); and Orestes asserts that a figurative beast's poison is literally deadly even when it does not bite (*Ch.* 994–96).

Thus, the distinction between figurative and literal vanishes, the complex sense of metaphors cannot be eliminated by interpretation that translates them into simpler, literal statements, and metaphors contaminate action with unwanted significance in the same way that oxymora do. In describing his army as a "beast," for example, Agamemnon apparently means simply that with an animal's god-given strength it has won a great victory (*Ag.* 821f.), but the figure itself means more than this because it expresses an identity, and an identity cannot hold only in part. The army is therefore bestial in every respect—savage, unrestrained by human law—and its compounded human, bestial nature makes its strength morally equivocal: the beast eats its victims (828), but, because it is also human, it must be judged in human terms for having consumed its own kind.[39] The complexity of action again corresponds to complexity in the gods, for the bestial army is (metaphorically) a "Fury" (55–59), an underworld deity that eats its victims (cf. *Eu.* 253) but is dispatched by Olympian Zeus, who seems to be located (metaphorically) "beneath the earth" (*Ag.* 1386f.).[40] Thus, there is a single complex Olympian and chthonic Zeus, and the army's savage pleasure, which unites *bia* and *kharis*, imitates his (metaphorically) "violent grace" (*kharis biaios*).[41]

The complexity of metaphors exceeds that of oxymora because, although both figures violate the conventional definitions of words, they are differently formed: the oxymoron asserts, for example, that *kharis* is not *kharis*, that something is not itself; the metaphor qualifies *kharis* as if it were something else (as *biaios*).[42] The oxymoron is self-contained; it consists in an internal contradiction, so that its context does not alter its meaning. The metaphor attacks the simple definition of words externally, ascribing to one the alien sense of another; it extends the possibilities of association, implicating simple things within its own complexity, so that its context enlarges its meaning. Metaphors, as a result, proliferate and combine in the *Agamemnon*, they produce a network of likeness and association that makes everything seem comparable to everything else.[43] This higher order of complexity becomes another source of difficulty for the dramatic characters. The difficulty is not confusion, however,[44] but an unforgiving system of justice that denies each human participant an unequivocal, distinct definition of himself, his separate identity. If oxymora reflect the substance of crime, the pollution of the Atreids, then metaphors embody the principle of its perpetuation, the sameness of the generations.

Iphigenia's sacrifice is a key incident. It is "another sacrifice" (*Ag.* 151), the implicit equivalent of prior events (including Thyestes' feast)[45] that are now seen metaphorically as sacrificial. This metaphorical redefinition of the past remakes Agamemnon into a substitute for his father and also for Thyestes: by killing a child, he commits Atreus's crime and in payment suffers Thyestes' loss; or, as Thyestes he punishes Atreus, and as Atreus he incriminates himself. The ease with which Aeschylean characters serve as substitutes for one another—as figurative signs magically identified with the things they signify—makes them commit the same actions again and again; crime replicates itself (produces *pleiona . . . eikota*, *Ag.* 758–60; cf. *Atan/ eidomenan tokeusin*, 771), and punishment replicates crime. Orestes invokes this pattern explicitly. He takes his father's place (*Ch.* 504) and his mother's: Clytemnestra deserves to die, according to the principle of like for like, and so, when

Orestes kills her, she "kills herself" according to the principle of metaphorical substitution (*Ch.* 923).[46] According to a different version of the same logical relationship, each Atreid connotes the others because all are identified in common with things larger and less distinct than any single person: Orestes wishes to be a "sign" of Zeus, like his father (*Ch.* 258f.), and Clytemnestra claims to be the "image" (*phantazomenos*, *Ag.* 1500) of the family's avenging spirit (*alastôr*).

There, is, then, a double problematic in the Atreid curse that corresponds to the two sorts of magically valid, figurative speech. As metaphors indicate, the Atreids' actions cannot be simply interpreted or simply judged—the curse continues—because they are never simply themselves and yet they never cease to be themselves in becoming something else; denotation cannot be isolated from connotation. Orestes, for example, must be judged in equal measure as what he is (his mother's son, a matricide) and as what he signifies or "stands for"[47] ("Clytemnestra," "Agamemnon," "Zeus"). And, as oxymora indicate, the Atreids cannot be simply judged because even the identity they share is equivocal, an identity formed from contradiction: they are criminals who violate their own nature, or else the nature of Zeus, opposing itself, has made them criminals. The end of the curse requires a way out of both kinds of complexity, metaphorical and oxymoronic. Each of the things equated in the first two plays of the trilogy must be separately defined, so that each may be judged in its own limited terms and therefore judged with an assurance of finality. (This chiefly depends upon defining Zeus as something distinct from his ubiquitous human "signs" or upon distinguishing the chosen, intended sense of human action from its larger connotation as the work of Zeus.) And then, if possible, the things separately defined must also be defined simply, without dysphemism, so that good can be summoned without concomitant evil. (This is a problem chiefly posed by the Furies, who leave the stage at the trilogy's end, accompanied by a call for "euphemism" [*Eu.* 1035, 1039].)

Zeus emerges as a distinct entity in the *Eumenides* when the Furies emerge as a distinct class that does not submit to comparison:

> . . . like no other race of creatures sown.   (410)

> . . . an uncanny band
> of women . . .
> or, rather, not women—I mean Gorgons;
> yet I shall not liken them to the Gorgons' shape . . .
> . . . these are wingless . . .
> I have not seen the tribe from which this fellowship
>   comes.   (46–58)

As a metaphorical creature in the *Agamemnon*, the Fury was the agent of Zeus, as Zeus was metaphorically god of the underworld (*Ag.* 55–59, 1386f.). Now, it seems, the herald's notion (*Ag.* 637) is confirmed, and Furies and Olympians do not mix (*Eu.* 69f.).[48]

The replacement of metaphorical Furies with real ones who are incomparable and resistant to the equivocations of metaphor catalyzes other distinctions, which replace other metaphorical equivocations. As female deities, the Furies serve Clytemnestra, who now appears as purely Mother, no longer the complex masculine-feminine creature she was in the *Agamemnon* (*Ag.* 11), and they are opposed by Apollo, who speaks for the father's specifically masculine rights (*Eu.* 658f.). They care only for the ties of blood, punishing those who kill their kin but defending criminals like Clytemnestra who violate the ties of marriage (*Eu.* 605, 211–22). Thus, the literal Furies would discount Paris's offense against marriage, the theft of Menelaus's wife, which was punished by a metaphorical Fury in the *Agamemnon*, and they would distinguish the theft of Helen from its metaphorical equivalent in the *Agamemnon*, revoking the image of Helen as a nestling stolen from its parents, which equates wife and child, marital ties and blood (*Ag.* 47–54).

The definition of Zeus, on the other hand, evokes a new distinction between life and death, and between binding and murder, a key point in the Olympian case as Apollo represents it. Since Zeus has bound his father, not killed him, his favor for the human father's rights cannot be faulted as inconsistent (*Eu.* 640–51); binding is curable, death is not (646–48). Fatal "binding" belongs only to the world ruled by the metaphorical "Zeus," whose human agent was a "Fury" and whose ally Night "bound" Troy (*Ag.* 55–59, 355–61). Now, however, the murder of Agamemnon and Cassandra can no longer be called "binding"[49] (cf. *Ag.* 1114f., *Ch.* 980f.). Therefore, in retrospect, the rite performed by Orestes and Electra in the *Choephoroe* to raise the spirit of Agamemnon, to make him live metaphorically in his son, seems vain. It produces figurative life for Agamemnon on the assumption that he was only figuratively slain. Since Agamemnon was literally slain (and not "bound"), he cannot survive in Orestes, and Orestes may no longer be regarded as a substitute for his father, guilty of his father's crimes. As Olympian justice has been simplified, stripped of connotation in the Athenian court of law, human identities and human actions have become more distinct.

But some of the *Agamemnon*'s equivocality persists in the *Eumenides* even after Zeus and the Olympians have been distinguished from the Furies, and so the simplification of justice must continue. The Furies retain their dangerous complexity; they emerge as the last champions of magical figures. Their deadly "binding song," for example, demonstrates the continued validity of the metaphor associated earlier with Zeus; vengeance, for the Furies, remains a "sacrifice";[50] and the "tuneless tune" of the *Agamemnon* (1142; cf. *Ch.* 822) may still be heard in their "lyreless hymn" (*Eu.* 344–46).

Appropriately, therefore, the Furies' eventual appeasement is confirmed by their cooperation in simplifying complex language. When Athena celebrates the triumphant emergence of their "*eris* (zeal) for good things" (*Eu.* 974f.), she offers—to an audience made sensitive to the sounds of words—the "true" (*etumos*) meaning of *Erinys* ("Fury"; cf. *Se.* 723–26). But *eris* normally connotes "strife" as well as "zeal"; its negative sense is shared by a synonym, *stasis*. Thus, when the Furies answer Athena's praise of *eris* by condemning *stasis* (976–79), they seem to distribute the two opposed qualities of *eris* between two distinct words: *stasis* alone bears the sense of "strife," and *eris* becomes unequivocally positive. In retrospect, this distinction denies that *eris* is "bloody" (*Ag.* 698, 1461) or "savage" (*Ch.* 474) and that the *Erinys* is "Strife" (*Stasis*, *Ag.* 1117, 1119); *Erinys* ("Fury") is now, in its "true" sense, an auspicious, euphemistic term.[51]

When the Furies are simplified, the elements of human experience are simplified also: *kharis* ceases to be *akharis* or *biaios* (*Eu.* 938–48), and song, no longer tuneless, becomes, by definition, the antithesis of sorrow (*Eu.* 954; cf. 346). In the ethical realm, right and wrong are distinguished (fulfilling the promise of *Eu.* 472, 488) and isolated from the complex amalgam created by the Atreids' justly patterned criminality (cf. *Ag.* 732, *Eu.* 554).[52] Finally, the repetition of crime ceases and the generations of men are distinguished because as the Furies are reduced to a distinct, literal identity, a concrete presence, they become "childless" (*apaides*, *Eu.* 1034),[53] incapable of producing more of their kind—like the "Fury" Agamemnon or the *alastôr* Clytemnestra—in the endless equations of metaphor. The meaning of action can now be controlled.

If the trilogy's language is magically valid from start to finish, the *Eumenides'* new definition of things as separate and distinct indicates a profound, objective change in the world inhabited by the dramatic characters, a change that eludes explanation because its only sign, the magical language, cannot itself be explained: according to Heraclitus, it "signifies" but does not "talk about" or clarify things (fr. 93). If the language is not magical, of course, it is reasonable to suppose that the figures of the *Agamemnon* are errors, that the dramatic world has not changed, and therefore that it gets all the explanation it needs from the correct literalism of the *Eumenides*. Orestes, for example, finally learns to recognize and to name things as they are, whereas Clytemnestra, in the grip of Delusion (*Atê*), knows the world only through metaphor and on that basis violates the rules of piety.[54] But if Clytemnestra is mistaken in naming "Zeus of the underworld," then the chorus must also be wrong to name a "Fury sent by Zeus," and Cassandra to call Agamemnon's death a sacrifice (*Ag.* 1118). The error would be the same in each case, to confuse Olympian Zeus with Hades. In the *Agamemnon*, however, there is no voice more reliable than these and no orthodoxy to protect Aeschylus's Athenian audience from reading the figures as facts.[55] Thus, it does not seem possible to distinguish the subjective from the objective element in the figures, to say that one is an error and that another, perhaps, is correct, just as it seems impossible to separate Agamemnon's choice at Aulis from the necessity he chooses.[56] The language used by the dramatic characters, like their behavior, is overdetermined, subjective and objective at the same time; it is a necessary choice, located at a point where intended and unintended meanings meet.

The remaining problem—the failure of magical language to explain what it signifies, the world's changing condition—is, perhaps, a problem for modern readers only. If Aeschylus's style is formed according to an exotic notion of language, the psychology of response appropriate to Aeschylean drama should be exotic too. Since magic unites words and object, one need only hear the word to perceive the object directly. Thus, magical speech, and the objects present in speech, may be apprehended without interpretive effort and without explanation of the kind needed to make absent things intelligible.[57] Aeschylus's style becomes for his listener an experience of substance,[58] its figures impose an experience of complexity, and the simple language of the *Eumenides* offers an "escape from troubles" (*apallagê ponôn*) strictly analogous to the one Orestes enjoys (83); in Hesiodic terms, Aeschylus allows his audience to "forget"[59] when the Atreids' "unforgetting" avenging spirit (*alastôr*) also apparently forgets, releasing Orestes, now purified, from his figurative responsibility for the past. Thus, if the *Eumenides* seems stylistically impoverished, this quality may be construed as the poet's way of freeing his audience from the fearsome world governed by metaphor. Having escaped by way of forgetfulness from a complex to a simple world, the audience requires no more explanation for its changed condition than the Furies require for their change of heart.

According to this argument, Aeschylus has deepened the significance of the identity between the form and content of poetry, an identity basic to Homeric poetics, and the result is a psychology of audiences that differs radically from Homer's. The truth of Homeric poetry is guaranteed by the automatic correspondence between language and its subject matter, but the norms of response depend upon neither of these things; Homer's audience is charmed by song, charmed precisely because song distinguishes itself from experience. In Aeschylean drama, the emotions of the audience are engaged as they are in the experience of life, not merely by the mimetic qualities of stage performance, which a modern audience expects, but by the affective power of style. Aeschylus's notion of language entails an act of singular courage on the poet's part and demands equal courage in the audience, for he is willing to make the drama of dangerous things dangerous itself, to evoke directly the hopeless, criminal complexity of the Furies' world. Aeschylus speaks where Pindar's pious care inspires silence, and before the purifying effects of forgetfulness may be enjoyed, his art induces an unpurified, indiscriminate, and frightening Memory.

INVISIBLE BODIES: GORGIAS,

ARISTOPHANES, AND EURIPIDES,

AND THE NATURE OF LANGUAGE

WHEN THE VALIDITY AND THE EFFICACY OF LAN-
guage is guaranteed, as it seems to be for the author of the
Oresteia, by a magical, homeopathic relationship to the
things of the world, the meaning of words is something
that need not, and cannot, be explained. Verbal ambiguity,
for example, must be regarded as an analogue of the ambivalence of things. Thus, ambiguous speech is apprehended most exactly when one abandons the effort to reduce language to order, to analyze it as though ambiguity
will disappear and clear, orderly truth will emerge, when
the proper, simple meaning of words has been fixed and
the key to the codes by which they are combined has been
discovered. Rather, because words possess the nature and
the structure of things, unmediated by any sort of artificial
grammar or syntax or rhetoric, and things are apprehended
through words directly, the obscurities of language are in-
escapable and true.

Discourse, as it is conducted in this sort of magical language, is a contest of competing spells in which each speaker's attempt to elicit the other's understanding and assent is
an attempt to enchant him. To a modern ear, the discourse
of enchantment seems inconsequential; issues are decided
convulsively, in complete revolutions of feeling and point
of view, as when the Furies at the end of the *Oresteia* stop
their brooding, indignant, hypnotically repetitive lamenta-
tions (*Eu.* 778–92 = 808–22; 837–46 = 870–80) and re-

mark, as though they themselves could scarcely understand it, that Athena's charm is working (*thelxein m'eoikas
kai methistamai kotou*, 900; cf. 885–87), that they have been
"displaced" from their anger. This sort of charming persuasion evokes a passive response from its object—the Furies
feel themselves changed—because its language is not interpreted as an argument but experienced as a thing. Arguments are apprehended analytically and may be partly
correct, partly mistaken, or partly accepted and partly dis-
puted; things may only exist or not and may be seen or ig-
nored. Incantations, which gain force by repetition (cf. *Eu.*
881) rather than rhetorical finesse, are like things in this respect: they win the mind's acquiescence by commanding
its attention or they fail to do both completely (the Furies
ignore Athena until they yield to her). Thus, the only way
to understand a magical speech is to feel it and yield to it;
the knowledge it conveys comes simultaneously with the
experience of the words, the perceived sound automatically carries its appropriate sense, and the affective and
cognitive aspects of listening coincide.

Aeschylus is perhaps the last of the Greek poets for
whom speech possesses something like a magical and unbroken connection to the things it describes, but notions
corollary to this primitive belief remain current much
longer;[1] in particular, a magical psychology of language becomes the subject of explicit theory among Greek authors
of the next generation. Its most basic form can be found in
the works of Gorgias, and it is adapted to the different requirements of their dramatic fictions by Aristophanes, in
the *Frogs*, and Euripides, in the *Helen*.

Gorgias insists (*On Nature* 84–86) that, because words
are physically different from things (*ta hupokeimena*), things
cannot be revealed in words; to describe an object entails a
translation from substance to speech that destroys the validity of speech. But Gorgias still regards speech, at least
metaphorically, as a substance, and he explains the psychology of verbal communication as a magical process that

derives its potency from the quasi-substantial nature of words: speech "accomplishes with the smallest and most invisible body (*sôma*) the most divine deeds" (*Helen* 8); it seems to enter the soul physically, the way a drug enters the flesh (14), and so it does its work irresistibly (12).

For Gorgias, words have all the psychic impact of things because they are, properly and exclusively, things of the mind, the only things directly perceived by it and apparently composed of the same notional material. Because the mind does not directly see real objects, real objects can never be known by the mind; it sees only impressions or "images" (*eikones*) relayed by the organs of sight, and these differ from real objects fundamentally. For example, the impressions linger timelessly, whether their objective source remains present or not (*Helen* 17). An opinion (*doxa*), something that "seems to be" (cf. *dokeô*) or a thing seen by "the eyes of opinion (*doxa*)" in the mind (13), has the same status as these *eikones*, except that *doxai* need not derive even indirectly from real objects.[2] But while impressions and opinions differ from real objects as words do, impressions and words do not differ from each other: the "remnants" of sensation are, according to Gorgias, "exactly like speech" (*homoia d' esti ta paraleipomena hoiaper ta legomena*, 17), and so words, like impressions, are directly present to the mind.[3]

This is the source of the "magical" power of speech. The mind ignores the gap between the impression of a sensation and the object from which sensation is derived because these impressions are the mind's only experience. Words are "exactly like" mental impressions because the mind also ignores the gap between words and things. Therefore, words are experienced as though they were things, not as signs that merely refer to things or describe them, and their direct and quasi-physical influence upon the mind does not depend upon their being understood or interpreted, upon the mind's ability to track down a referent through the words that denote it. The words do all the work themselves, and the mind is passive. Thus, incantation, which can evidently produce its effect without being understood, seems typical of speech in general: it has a charm (*thelxis*) that changes what the mind sees (*doxa*) by "mingling with it" (*sungignomenê*, *Helen* 10). And because words, in this elementary way, bypass interpretation or understanding, they are able to make "visible" (*phainesthai*) even things that are unintelligible or, by a rational standard, unbelievable (13).

The process of persuasion as Gorgias envisions it has often been called irrational,[4] but perhaps it can be defined less invidiously as nonanalytical or analogical. Since words are experienced immediately as things and not as references to things, sentences composed of words should possess no mediating syntactic or grammatical structure that must be deciphered to be grasped. Instead, according to Gorgias, they have something like a shape, which affects the soul, as sensation does, by "stamping" it (*hê peithô . . . tên psukhên etupôsato*, *Helen* 13; cf. 15).[5] The effect is an analogue of the words themselves, unmediated by analysis of linguistic structure on the listener's part.

The difference between language viewed as a structured system of signs and language viewed as a thing may be compared to the difference between a mathematical description of musical sounds and the sounds themselves: the same information is contained in both, but sounds are not coded in a way that requires analysis and interpretation (and few people would claim to hear or enjoy the mathematical formulas). In fact, in Gorgias's account, language works in much the same way as music seems to do according to his contemporary, Damon.[6] Damon describes the ethical qualities of music, its ability to form the listener's moral character (fr. 6); "feminine" sound makes feminine souls, "masculine" sound masculine souls, for example (fr. 7), and when musical "modes" (*tropoi*) change, civic customs (*nomoi*) do also (fr. 10). Evidently, sounds do not signify or refer to ethical qualities—they convey these qualities simply by possessing them, by being masculine or feminine, courageous, just, and moderate, or the reverse; their effect arises from their nature as things rather than their meaning as signs. Taken together, Gorgias's claim (that words have something like the direct impact of music) and Damon's (that music possesses ethical qualities normally associated with speech) make music and speech nearly indistinguishable, and this is precisely what one would expect as a result of the joint evolution of verbal and musical art in Greek poetry. The psychological theories newly elaborated in the second half of the fifth century are based upon a tradition of poets like Pindar, who describes his work as a species of song.[7]

But there is a difference between Gorgias's theory and traditional views of poetry which follows from his insistence that words are more immediately present to the mind than physical objects apprehended by the senses, and from his rejection of the primitive belief that the relationship between words and physical objects is naturally fixed, that words magically reflect the truth: because words (even when they are truthful) differ essentially from real things but are experienced as real by the mind, they deceive in all their uses.[8] Thus, Homeric enchantment (*thelxis*), which seduces the poet's audience into an alien perspective, and philosophical argument (*Helen* 13), which alters what the mind sees (*doxa*), have become the same deceptive art, *apatê*.[9] For Homer, poetry is true but not psychically real, for Gorgias psychically real but not necessarily true, and in this reversal poetry loses its special status as a medium in which the experiences of life are set at a distance, transformed, and purified. Rather, it has the power of all speech to evoke the feelings proper to personal experience— terror, pity, and a "yearning to lament" (*pothos philopenthês*, 9)—so that upon hearing about the sufferings of others, the listener's soul suffers its own (*idion ti pathêma*, 9).

It seems likely that when Gorgias calls tragedy "deception" (fr. 23), he means simply that it possesses the power of any verbal art to counterfeit experience and not that it creates an illusion peculiar to the theater.[10] Since all speech deceives, there should be no large difference in the psychic effects of first and third person narration or in those of narration and dramatic impersonation.[11] And since the deceptions of speech are not necessarily untruthful, there is nothing paradoxical in Gorgias's claim that a spectator who is deceived by tragedy is "wiser" than one who is not; on the contrary, the mind unaffected and undeceived by speech ignores its proper environment of notional, nonphysical things.

Thus, the report that Gorgias admired Aeschylus (fr. 24) seems plausible, despite the relatively weak illusionism of Aeschylus's plays. Gorgias's psychology of verbal magic is at least compatible with the magical status of language and with its rhetorical use in the *Oresteia*, and this compatibility is exploited by Aristophanes, who associates Gorgianic views with Aeschylus in the *Frogs*.[12] The *Frogs* explores the aesthetic and moral implications of the psychology of words experienced as things by setting it in conflict with another, more modern view that is represented by a fictional Euripides, whose psychology, aesthetics, and morality are based upon a formal and analytical notion of language.

The two linguistic theories surface at the penultimate stage of the contest, when the poets' words are weighed on a scale. Aeschylus wins this trial, of course, because "heaviness" is his strength and his weakness: Euripides has "slimmed" the language of poetry, Aeschylus has made it bloated (*Frogs* 939–43). He wins also because the test of weight reflects, with the distortions of Aristophanic parody, the Gorgianic notion that words are like things, a premise more congenial to Aeschylus's art than to Euripides'. Gorgias's theory at least accounts for the psychological weight of words such as "death" (1392); another notion, primitive and, at the end of the fifth century, absurd, makes words such as "river" (1383) share the physical nature of the things they represent. "Death" tips the scale because physical and psychological weight are equated here, the Gorgianic theory confounded with its primitive counterpart, and the metaphor of one made the literal truth of the other.

Euripides' loss in the test of weight dramatizes what Aeschylus regards as the weakness of Euripides' art, its spiritual insubstantiality. Euripides' words have no weight because they are nothing but words, pure language without sense. For example, when Euripides puts "persuasion" in the scales, it weighs little because it has no "mind" (*nous*, 1396). His creative organ, and the god he worships, is the tongue (826f., 892), but Aeschylus produces speech from deep within himself, with the breath of his lungs (829).[13] The language of the tongue has become an independent entity, and so it can be manipulated according to formal criteria alone, polished and refined (819), but Aeschylus's language, as a direct, unmediated expression of the spirit,[14] issues forth ready-made and "shaggy" and refuses to submit to formal aesthetic standards. For a similar reason, perhaps, Aeschylus's language, and not Euripides', is "equal" (*isa*) to the thoughts it expresses (1058f.).[15] And although Aeschylus can only say what he feels, Euripides has made possible a new insincerity by emptying verbal forms. Thus, he deserves to be betrayed by Dionysus, who swore to rescue him but swore only with his tongue, like Euripides' character Hippolytus (1471; cf. *Hipp.* 612). According to Aeschylus, Euripides' poetry has taught the Athenians a sort of dishonesty (1083–88) that is the reverse of Gorgianic deception, a dishonesty based upon the separation rather than the identity of speech and feeling.

It follows that since Euripidean language has been divided at its origin from the spirit and made empty form, it is also unable to inspire the souls of an audience with pleasure, which Aeschylus regards as poetry's proper effect. Thus, although Dionysus begins his journey to the under-

world with an ambiguously intellectual and sensual passion[16] for Euripides, he comes finally to prefer Aeschylus
because he feels the spiritual pleasure Aeschylus offers
and because he judges finally with his soul (1468), the
organ to which Aeschylean poetry addresses itself, not
with his intellect or his senses.[17] With the soul's pleasure in
language, Dionysus elevates a Gorgianic principle,[18] as he
punishes Euripides for having violated one in withholding
pleasure by separating language from the soul.

The measure of creativity, another standard by which
the poets are judged, also depends upon poetry's spiritual
substance. As Dionysus searches for a "productive" or
"fertile" poet (*gonimos*, 96),[19] one who produces "noble" or
"well-born" speech (*gennaion rhêma*, 97), it seems at first
that Euripides meets his requirements, for Euripides' language is novel and adventurous (*parakekinduneumenon*, 99),
sophisticated because it differs from the ordinary (906). But
Euripides brings to birth mere words, "chatter" as it is
practiced by idle young men, which lacks both the simplicity and the moral content of old-fashioned speech.[20]
The absence of moral content, like the absence of pleasure,
suggests that Euripidean poetry has nothing to do with the
soul; it does not come from the poet's soul or affect the
souls of his audience. Therefore, if language is measured
in spiritual terms, Euripides has created nothing of substance. Aeschylus, on the other hand, introduces fictional
characters who "breathe" spears and helmets (1016), whose
souls are dense with the presence of things; his poetry has
spirit and the spirit has substance. The chant of men rowing, which he cites as an example of morally sound speech,
is clearly neither sophisticated nor original; it is repetitive
and unintelligible as language.[21] But its virtue consists in its
ability to strengthen and unite men in action, and therefore, in spiritual terms, the poet who produces something
like this chant truly creates.[22] This is Aeschylus's title to the
character that Aristophanes gives him as a bull (804), a

creature of supreme sexual vigor,[23] and as a madman (816), overflowing with feeling, overstocked with the substance of the spirit.

Euripides, however, implicitly rejects Aeschylus's notion of language as a spiritual substance, and so he accepts none of the judgments against him that are directly or indirectly associated with it. His own account of the function of language, and of the virtues and vices of poetry, assumes that words are not things in themselves and do not properly possess the qualities of things; they are rather signs of things, which transmit information only by referring to things, ideally in the most economical and precise manner (1178). Aeschylus's poetry, according to this view, scarcely even attempts to communicate, although it pretends to do so, and its failure or its perversity is typified by its emotionally laden silences (915–20), which convey nothing that can be called information because they do not refer to anything. Almost as bad as silence are words unknown to the audience (*agnôta*, 926) because they do not refer to things clearly (927, 1122) or intelligibly (*ha xumbalein ou rhadi' ên*, 930; cf. 959) and words that denote nonexistent things like the "goat-deer" (*tragelaphos*, 937) because they refer clearly to nothing: in all cases, there is a failure of reference. Euripides' own language, on the other hand, is characterized by its "correctness" (*orthotês tôn epôn*, 1181),[24] that is, by its precision of reference. He will not, for example, use two words with the same meaning together, as Aeschylus does (1154, 1173f., 1178f.), for this violates the standard of "correctness" by failing to take account of what words signify.

The value Euripides places upon dramatically representing familiar, everyday situations (959) may be explained, according to this principle, as a reflection of his desire to refer clearly to real things, for the familiar is most certainly real, and the discussion of familiar things by the dramatic characters will be most readily understood by an audience (*hois xunesmen*, 959). Since language that functions as a reference to things must be deciphered and things must be identified indirectly, it is most intelligible when its referents are known in advance, and intelligible to the largest number of people when its referents are known most widely. And the representation of familiar things leaves intact the audience's ability to perform the activity of deciphering and construing what it hears: it does not "amaze" (*ekplêt-tein*, 962)[25] and so take away the power of thought (*to phronein*, 962); Aeschylean bombast, on the other hand, requires and allows no knowledge or mental activity in its audience because it need only be felt, not understood. Intellect and Tongue, Euripides' gods, complement one another (892f.).

While the Euripidean audience must be active, rather than passive, and emotionally detached from the drama, rather than inspired, because it has a task of understanding to perform in the theater, the poet, conversely, relinquishes his power to create, to be spiritually *gonimos*, so that he may take on the humbler task of describing. Anything else, according to Euripides, is a form of deception (*apatê*, 909f.; cf. 921), a deception conceived roughly in the terms of Gorgianic psychology as the power of language to make of itself an experience for its listeners rather than to signify or describe. Thus, there are two kinds of deception in the *Frogs*, Euripides' insincerity and Aeschylus's Gorgianic emotionalism, here regarded as a fault; one separates language from the spirit, the other identifies them too closely.

The alternative to Aeschylean creativity, which makes a counterfeit and deceptive experience out of words, is "skill" (*dexiotês*), the quality Euripides claims for himself and wishes to test in his opponent (1121), which aims at formal, purely verbal invention (cf. *lepton*, 1108, 1111). This undeceiving virtue is explicitly associated with the use of books,[26] and so it is possible to see the poets' argument as a reflection of a larger conflict between oral and literate cultures or between two generations,[27] the first of which has encountered poetry almost exclusively through recitation, the second having learned to retrieve its meaning through the abstract and highly formalized code of the phonetic alphabet.[28] Among the latter, for example, Thucydides disdains the pleasure speech offers its audience and prefers the truth clearly and impersonally preserved in the written word (1.22.4), whereas Plato's Socrates revives the older values and echoes Aeschylus in preferring madness (*mania*) and sincerity (*spoudê*) in speech[29] to the inauthentic discipline of writing.[30] In Socrates' view, only the spoken word is "alive," informed with the soul's breath (*empsukhos*) as Aeschylus would have it.[31]

Euripides and Aeschylus agree about one thing, that poets should make men better "in the cities" (1008–12),[32] but their views about moral and political life differ as radically, and in the same way, as their views about language and the psychology of communication. As Aeschylus accounts for the process, moral character is transmitted directly to the passive soul: as the soul is "stamped" and its characteristics (*tropoi*) changed by speech and by the impressions of sense in Gorgianic psychology (*Helen* 13, 15), Aeschylus claims to have been "molded" (*apomaxamenê*, 1040) by his knowledge of Lamachus, whom he regards as a civic hero and an appropriate model for other citizens to imitate. And it is reasonable to suppose that Aeschylus in turn has imposed his moral stamp upon the city with his plays, that his influence reproduces its source ("out of nobility and into nobility," 1298), because Aristophanes, speaking for himself in the parabasis of the *Frogs*, describes the best citizens as good "coinage" (718–22) formed under the influence of dance, music, and virile games,[33] and now lamentably displaced in public life by men "struck with the most degraded die" (*kopeisi tôi kakistôi kommati*, 726).[34] Since men will tend to take on the qualities of whatever they see around them in the city or on the stage, a poet teaches evil simply by representing or describing it,[35] his judgments or arguments about what he presents notwithstanding. This is the basis for Aeschylus's charge that the erotic adventures of Euripidean women will ruin the women of Athens: the poet must "conceal—not dramatize, not teach—what is wicked" (1053f.).[36]

Euripides seems more puzzled by this than offended (cf. 1049); he merely objects that the stories he has told are true, that the things he represents really exist (*onta*, 1052), and so he apparently does not believe that a true story should be harmful to its audience or that the audience must reproduce what it is given to contemplate. The familiar, domestic matters he presents on stage are not meant to mold souls but to provide the material and the methods of analysis (959ff.), just as the language his characters use serves as a tool of the intellect, applied to reveal more precisely the reality evoked in his plays.

Therefore, in the moral virtues Aeschylus claims for himself, Euripides sees only an aesthetic flaw, as Euripides' aesthetic virtues are moral flaws by Aeschylus's standards, and this difference between them follows from the others. Because Aeschylus believes that the moral qualities of poetry reproduce themselves directly in the souls of the audience, he approaches his single goal, to foster virtue, through a single, undifferentiated, virtuous medium. Thus, as his dramatic characters must be always noble, his diction (1059–62; cf. 1004f.) and his music must be always noble too, so as not to diminish the improving effects of the play.[37] The variety of Euripidean odes, according to this criterion, is as morally suspect as adultery in his plots:[38] his indiscriminate writing (*apo pantôn*, 1301) suggests the indiscriminate behavior of criminals (*panourgoi*: cf. 80, 781, 1520), his many lyric devices suggest the inventiveness of a whore (1327).[39] But for Euripides, Aeschylus's selectiveness and homogeneity are simply tedious and repetitive, "always the same thing" (1250).

The moral terms of this argument about the influence of poetry translate directly into political ones. For example, Aeschylus's moral selectivity in choosing his literary mate-

rial corresponds to a conservative antipathy toward allow-
ing new human material, especially slaves and foreigners,
into Athenian civic life, and Euripides' artistic promiscuity,
like his alleged dependence upon the slave Cephisophon
(944, 1408, 1452), associates him with the rising under-
class.[40] But the most important political question concerns
the power of the poet and the distribution of power in the
city that his literary behavior implicitly favors. This problem underlies the last, apparently decisive stage of the contest between Aeschylus and Euripides, and it offers the
best approach to what Aristophanes may have thought
about his own role, as a poet practicing his art in Athens in
the absence of both of the two contending tragedians.

In Aristophanes' fancy, the deceptively impressive, portentous language of Aeschylus also belongs to a certain
sort of Athenian public orator[41] and especially to Pericles:
both Aeschylus and Pericles overwhelm Greece like a
storm, confounding everything with thunder and lightning, achieving a power over their passive audiences that
resembles the power of Olympian Zeus.[42] Their affinity
seems natural, for Pericles' abilities, as Thucydides describes them and as they are likely to have been understood by Athenians generally, are those that belong traditionally to poets and, in Gorgias's account, to all who use
the *logos* successfully. Like Homer, Hesiod, and Pindar,
Pericles could divert his listeners from the present (*apo tôn
parontôn deinôn apagein tên gnômên*, Thuc. 2.65.1) and ma-
nipulate their emotions, change their confidence to fear
and their fear to confidence (2.65.8–9; cf. *Helen* 14) with
a sudden irrational overturn (*kataplêxis*, 2.65.9) like the
"amazement" of Gorgias (*ekplêxis*, *Helen* 16) and Aeschylus
(*Frogs* 962).

There is a political virtue in this art, to which Aeschylus
has surely a better claim than Euripides. By distracting his
fellow citizens from the present, Pericles was able to make
them take the longer and larger view, so that under his
guidance they avoided the errors they made after his death

in setting private gain over the welfare of the city (Thuc. 2.65.7). Thus, in governing a democracy, Hesiod's and Pindar's art of inducing forgetfulness of the present, the painful, and the mundane becomes a tool for maintaining unity against divisive private interests. Perhaps the justice of Gorgias's deceiving poet (fr. 23) also consists in creating a consensus of this sort, the shared *doxa* required for successful social life, for the psychic material upon which "amazement" acts includes the common habits of custom (*sunêtheia tou nomou, Helen* 16).[43] This is certainly the aim of Aristophanes' Aeschylus, who boasts that his single-minded art inspires every spectator alike (*Frogs* 1022).[44]

Euripides' art, which exercises no formative influence over its audience, fosters an equality of active intellectual competence rather than passive acquiescence (954ff.). Thus, it seems more democratic in spirit (cf. 952) but divisive in its effects, for its lessons concern the spectator's private affairs (*oikeia pragmata*, 959; cf. 976) and apparently nothing else. The lack of a communal center in Euripides' work is radical: even his gods are private (*idiôtai theoi*, 891), created by the poet himself without regard for established religious practice,[45] and they are gods of the verbal skills that support each man's rational pursuit of his own interest.[46] Evidently, then, Euripides belongs politically to the contentious post-Periclean age, when the Athenians, "now more equal to one another," pursued "private ambitions and private profit" (Thuc. 2.65.10; 2.65.7), and his quarrel with Aeschylus shows that Pericles' program has disintegrated: the democratic distribution of intellectual activity (2.40.2) seems no longer compatible with social cooperation, if it ever was.

In choosing to take Aeschylus back to Athens, Dionysus apparently expresses his approval of the poet's literary and political affinity to Pericles; at least his decision immediately follows Aeschylus's suggestion that the Athenians revive Pericles' military policy of twenty-five years before.[47] But in fact the criterion of choice remains far from clear, and its obscurity suggests Aristophanes' own ambivalence about the matter. Dionysus solicits the poets' views about Alcibiades and the salvation of Athens; he praises both for their responses, Aeschylus with perhaps more skepticism than enthusiasm; and finally he chooses Aeschylus as his "soul wishes" (1468). In the absence of an explicit link between the last stage of the contest and its outcome, one may wonder what the point of the questioning might be and, in particular, what the introduction of Alcibiades as a touchstone signifies.[48]

This problem is not precisely the same as the one Aristophanes addresses in the parabasis because the good citizens (khrêstoi, 735) to be rehabilitated in public life are the oligarchs of 411 or their associates, whereas Alcibiades seems dangerous in the popular imagination, not as an oligarch[49] but as a potential tyrant, a figure regarded by conservatives as a byproduct of democracy, hostile to themselves and to what they regard as freedom.[50] In this light, Aeschylus's complacency seems remarkable when he advises that once Alcibiades "the lion cub" (1431) has been allowed to grow and flourish, "it is necessary to serve his ways" (1433). But the poet merely remains true to his own principles, for his art associates him with Pericles, and Pericles can seem distinctly tyrannical to disenchanted eyes.[51] Alcibiades in turn is Pericles' heir, a lion cub in the Frogs because Pericles, according to a popular story, appeared as a lion to his mother in a dream.[52] This portent had already been associated, in Aristophanes' hands, with the type of the demagogue who wished to replace Pericles;[53] the deceptive language of Gorgias, mastered first by Aeschylus and Pericles, is handed down to Cleon.[54] Like Aeschylus (Frogs 814), Pericles, "the Olympian, stirred up Greece with thunder and lightning" (êstrapt' ebronta xunekuka tên Hellada, Acharn. 530f.); like Pericles, Cleon (the "Paphlagonian" of the Knights) "hurled forth words like thunder" (elasibront' anarrêgnus epê, Knights 626), "stirring everything up and mixing it together" (tarattôn kai kukôn,

Knights 692). The pattern of them all is Zeus, the tyrant of *Prometheus Bound*, whom Prometheus summons in defiance to "stir everything up with thunder and mix it together" (*brontêmasi/ khthoniois kukatô panta kai tarassetô*, *PB* 994f.).[55] Thus, the notion of "service" to Alcibiades hints at a darker side of Aeschylean poetics, with its passive, unthinking audience molded by a master of words,[56] and a darker side of Periclean leadership, especially in its later, degenerate form, as practiced by the warlike leaders of the people and by Alcibiades.

The uneasiness and indecision generated by Alcibiades in the *Frogs* no doubt reflects a more fundamental anxiety about the future of Athens, a sense that there are no remedies for the city's ills that are not themselves dangerous. But more to the point of the contest between poets, the last round of questioning suggests that in making Aeschylus the victor, Aristophanes has been forced to sacrifice something of his own comic art,[57] its distanced, unconfounded and unconfounding satirical clarity. Aeschylus's drama is "full of Ares" (1021), like his militant policies, and descends directly from the aggressive Lamachus (1039–42); Euripides' suspicion of patriotic bombast echoes the ridicule with which Aristophanes himself treated Lamachus and the war at least twenty years earlier, in the *Acharnians*. What Aeschylus regards as tragedy's duty, to adorn the noble deed (*kosmein ergon ariston*, 1027) as a model for imitation, seems, in the comic perspective of both the *Frogs* and the *Acharnians*, an endemic folly of the art, to adorn nonsense (*kosmein tragikon lêron*, *Frogs* 1005). There is nonsense in comedy too, but comic nonsense is hostile to the pretentious Aeschylean sort. It is closer to the wit of Euripides when he advises, in the best Aristophanic manner, turning one skinny Athenian into wings for another and sending them off to bomb the enemy from the air with vinegar (1437–42). The victory of Aeschylus eclipses this refreshing vision.

If Aristophanes does not wholeheartedly endorse Aes-

chylean art and the political values associated with it, perhaps he might remain faithful to himself by adopting it as
part of an ideal synthesis, an art that possesses the virtues
and is free of the vices of both tragic poets; the best poetry,
composed in a language of the spirit intelligible to the
mind, might produce a populace thoughtful and free, but
unified and courageous. Instead, the ambivalence underlying the last scene of the *Frogs* causes confusion, and the
categories by which the poets are defined collapse,[58] as if
Aristophanes, lacking a satisfactory answer to the questions he has raised, wished to extricate himself, leaving at
least the impression of differences resolved. Thus, Euripides and Aeschylus offer essentially the same advice for
saving the city, Aristophanes' own advice as it was expressed in the parabasis (734f., 1446–50; cf. 1454–59), and
each acquires the other's virtues and faults: Euripides displays unselfish patriotism (1429), pretentiousness (by association with the *semnoi logoi* of philosophers, 1496; cf. 833),
and obscurity (1444f.), Aeschylus a selfish reluctance to
help the city (1461) and the "exact intelligence" of the sophists (*xunesis êkribômenê*, 1483).[59]

The dialectic of the *Frogs* consumes itself and ends in dis-
array because a true synthesis of the two tragic arts lies beyond the dialectic's scope, in comedy. Thus, when Aristophanes praises himself, he claims a complete inventory
of Aeschylean and Euripidean virtues: he is clever, like Euripides' friends the sophists (*sophizomai*, *Clouds* 547), and
never deceives his audience by saying the same thing twice
(*Clouds* 546f., *Wasps* 1051–54); on the other hand, he does
not teach trickery and dirty dealing (cf. *Acharn.* 657f.)
but elevates his art, removing what is base and building
a grand edifice of thought and form (*Peace* 749f.), like Aeschylus (*Frogs* 1004), to foster an audience of uncomplaining
sailors (*Wasps* 1094ff.; cf. *Frogs* 1071f.).[60] In brief, Aristophanes unites the language of Euripides' poetry, for its precision and efficiency, with the substance of Aeschylus's, for

its better than common vision: "I use [Euripides'] terseness, but make the thoughts less mean" (fr. 471).[61]

Judged by the standard of comedy, Aeschylus's victory may be justified not for its intrinsic validity but for what it can contribute to the synthesis left uncompleted in the *Frogs*. If the ideally balanced art cannot be found in tragedy, perhaps tragedy's unresolved internal contradictions can produce a balanced set of skills and sensibilities in its audience by exerting distinct, competing influences. This seems to be Dionysus's purpose, for in resurrecting Aeschylus he ensures that the contest of the *Frogs* will continue: Aeschylus will return to a city "mad" about Euripides, as Dionysus was (103; cf. 776), to marshal the influence of his own art against the dominant modern ethos, and so to inform, if possible, its critical intellect with manly virtue. Dionysus himself has become the first member of this future audience in accepting Aeschylus without abandoning Euripides' critical reserve.[62] Thus, the partial, qualified validity of the *Frogs'* conclusion complements the partiality of its audience, and its sense is to be found in an implied, desired whole.

The dialectic of the *Frogs* begins logically with two disparate theories of language and ends with the question of poetry's relation to the world of practical necessity: since Aeschylus's poetry claims the power to create the substance of experience independently of the world because poetry need not signify, describe, or refer to anything in the world, it neglects practical concerns. These are at best extrinsic, and at worst destructive, to its self-contained spirit, hence Aeschylus's untempered artistic self-indulgence (*authadôs semnunomenos*, *Frogs* 1020; cf. 837), his carelessness of realism, his reluctance to answer Dionysus's specific queries, and the patent impracticality of his Themistoclean-Periclean military strategy, a spiritual rather than realistic response to present Athenian needs. Radi-

cally reduced, this posture becomes a rejection of everything but speech and the spirit. No use of language other
than the purely spiritual makes sense, according to Gorgias, because even if the world can be known, knowledge
about it cannot be communicated (*On Nature* 83–86); thus,
the master of words, who controls only *doxa*, an "insecure
thing" (*Helen* 11), nevertheless exercises irresistible power
and need concern himself with nothing else.

The Aristophanic Aeschylus merely disdains reality, but
Euripides' *Helen* seems to be based upon a more extreme
version of Gorgianic principles: if knowledge of the world
consists in nothing but *doxa*, the makers of *doxa*, as far as
we shall ever know or care, effectively make the world.
The deception of poets has become truly a divine force;[63] it
works unchecked by reality because reality remains always equivocal, and so it is freed from the dialectic of the
Frogs, which is haunted by the palpable, particular dangers
Athens faces. Euripides elsewhere seems more closely concerned with questions of the sort raised by Aristophanes.
Because the *Helen* is relatively systematic in working out its
esoteric premise and is untouched by any sense of poetry's
need to come to terms with things beyond its control, it occupies a special place among Euripides' other plays. But
within the limits imposed by its Gorgianic assumptions,
the *Helen* makes a significant attempt to recast the traditional poetic psychology of Homer, Hesiod, and Pindar in
the light of contemporary philosophy.

The basic condition of life in the play is that appearance
does not correspond to reality and words do not correspond, in any obvious way, to the things they are supposed to represent. For almost every issue of importance,
the *logos* given is subject to doubt, or there are two *logoi*
between which the dramatic characters have no means of
rational choice: Zeus in the form of a swan engendered
Helen, or perhaps he did not (17–21);[64] the Dioscuri are
dead and not dead (*duô d' eston logô*, 138); Menelaus is said
to be dead (132) but perhaps falsely (cf. 309).[65] And just as

there are multiple *logoi* about each thing, more than one thing is denoted by each single word: thus, Helen and her simulacrum are both called "Helen" (cf. 588), and there may be more than one being called "Zeus" (491–99).[66]

The precision that Prodicus and the Aristophanic Euripides want in language is therefore unobtainable, and the sophists' method of arguing according to probability[67] presupposes an uncertain, if not misleading, standard of truth. In the *Helen*, "clarity" depends upon both precision and probability, but nothing is ever "clear among men" (1148f.). The story of Menelaus's death, for example, seems "intelligible" to Helen (cf. *asuneta*, 352) and "clearly" told (308); it predicates something probable, but false, about someone unequivocally denoted.[68] The story of Helen's faithlessness seems clear to Menelaus, and when he meets his wife in Egypt, this "clarity" slips away from him (577); in fact, the story is true, but true of the phantasm equivocally called "Helen."[69]

This phantasm, of course, undermines the reality of appearances as its name undermines the clarity of words. Troy is destroyed and the Achaeans die for the image of Helen, a breathing, visible likeness (*eidôlon*) of the woman herself; they believe what they see as they believe what they hear, and the two causes of their delusion are strictly equivalent, for they struggle in either case for an "empty seeming" (*kenên dokêsin*, 36), which encompasses both the *eidôlon* of Helen and her "name" (*onoma*, 43).[70] The *eidôlon*, then, is the word's visible counterpart, at least in its effects, and closer examination of its nature suggests that it may serve as a model for language in other respects as well.

The *eidôlon* is partly alive, partly not; it has breath (*empnous*, 34) but no other, more solid physical substance (cf. 36). Although it must have seemed palpable to Menelaus and Paris, the *eidôlon* is at best a substitute for an absent person, and in this it resembles the statue of Alcestis[71] that Admetus will take to bed, calling it by his wife's name, thinking he has her when he does not (*Alc.* 348–54). The *eidôlon* is a statue too (*agalma*, *Helen* 705, 1219), a ritual token of the person it represents.[72] It makes little difference whether such a thing is insubstantial but endowed with living breath, like an *eidôlon*, or substantial but lifeless and cold, like the figure of Alcestis, for the nature of both is ambivalent, uncertainly placed between life and death. They are ghostlike, most vividly apprehended by living men in sleep,[73] and so, in the *Phoenician Women*, when Oedipus is ruined, metaphorically dead but physically alive, he calls himself an invisible *eidôlon* of aithêr or a winged vision of dreams (1543–45). *Aithêr*, which seems to be the substance of Helen's *eidôlon* too (cf. *Helen* 34), shares the *eidôlon*'s ambivalent nature, for *aithêr* is both the source of its breath and the place of dead souls.[74]

Helen's status in Egypt is therefore appropriately represented as that of a captive in Hades, whose *sôma* is rooted to the Egyptian earth while her *eidôlon* or ghost wanders where her *onoma* is invoked among the living. Like Persephone, she was taken while she gathered flowers[75] and was carried to Egypt by Hermes, guide of the dead. The house of Theoclymenus, the Egyptian king, is named, with a pun, the house of Plutus, lord of the underworld (69), and Helen is wooed by Theoclymenus as Persephone was wooed by Hades; when Helen invokes Persephone to send the Sirens, daughters of Earth (167–78), to join her lament, she is answered immediately by the chorus of the play as if the Sirens had indeed joined her.[76]

As the soul of Helen who is figuratively dead, the *eidôlon* is more than a copy or an image, and its deceptiveness is not the result of some inaccuracy of imitation but of the equivocality of its nature. The *eidôlon*, like the name, properly belongs to the person, and it deceives only when it is mistaken for a whole being, fully present in body and soul. Thus, when Odysseus cannot embrace his mother in the underworld and complains that Persephone has sent an *eidôlon* to grieve him, he must be corrected: in the underworld, an empty shape is no deceit; "Persephone . . . does not trick you,/ but this is the way of mortal men, when someone dies. For the sinews no longer have flesh and bones/ . . . but the soul flies away like a dream" (*Od.* 11.216–22).

Helen's *eidôlon*, therefore, is not necessarily false; it can be truly (if never really) "Helen," [77] and its truth or falsity is of the same type as truth and falsity in speech. (On the assumption that speech accurately reflects the nature of the speaker, Isocrates calls it an *eidôlon* of the soul.) [78] If it is perceived as real, however—and in Euripides' *Helen* this seems inevitable—the *eidôlon* deceives just as words inevitably and irresistibly deceive according to Gorgias: the "invisible body" of words, their equivocal reality directly experienced by the soul, and the ethereal substance of the *eidôlon*, urgently desired by Paris and Menelaus, exist in precisely the same way, as things composed of psychic, spiritual matter. According to Euripides, the source of both is some ethereal place in the sky (cf. fr. 978).

Thus, it makes sense that among the dead souls in Hades, as Aristophanes imagines them, where all substance is ethereal (cf. *Od.* 11), the words of poets may be weighed. And if the substance of words gives them divine power, according to Gorgias, it makes sense too that the substance of Helen's *eidôlon* must be formed by Hera, in a divine act of creation. [79] The *eidôlon* fits nicely into a gap left by Gorgianic psychology, which can find nothing in the phenomenal world that possesses the immediacy of speech. While real things must first be sensed and then the lingering sensations experienced by the soul, the *eidôlon*, like language, bypasses the senses so that Paris may feel Helen's living body within his empty embrace. In the theater, the *eidôlon* would enlarge the scope of Gorgianic *apatê* so that the visible action as well as the language of a play would be magically impressive: the figures on stage, if the poet should succeed in making them like *eidôla*, would be perceived more vividly than figures encountered in the course of daily life; spectators would see them as they see a vision in a dream, as if from within their own souls.

To make an *eidôlon*, of course, the poet must be godlike, and divinity will come within his reach only if he can free himself for a time from the confused perceptions of other men and know the *eidôlon* for what it is. As a source of knowledge, the vividly perceived but equivocal reality of the *eidôlon* may be compared to more common phenomena, unequivocally real but obscurely and ambiguously perceived. Thus, when Teucer meets Helen in Egypt after he has seen the *eidôlon* at Troy, he accepts the reality of both (118) but insists upon calling the *eidôlon* "Helen"; his mind (*nous*) "sees" no more and no less than his eyes (122), and so it depends for knowledge entirely upon appearance. Certainty, by contrast, is divine: when Helen identifies Menelaus despite his rags, she experiences her sudden insight as an epiphany, and she hails "recognition" (*to gignôskein*) as a god (560), a thing that comes unbidden and uncontrolled from some external source. Vulnerability to appearances is the condition described as universal and incurable by Gorgias, who apparently sees no need to explain how masters of language and seeming like himself can control appearances actively while other men suffer them passively. Euripides, however, elaborates Gorgianic psychology by adding to it another term, and he discovers in the human soul something that transcends the passive *nous*, with a power commensurate to the "most divine effects" of the *logos*.

The *nous* dies with the body, the mortal part of man,[80] but the "judgment" (*gnômê*; cf. *to gignôskein*) lives on, mingling with *aithêr* (1014–16) as like with like.[81] Since prophecy, according to the messenger in this play, was no help to the princes at Troy when they fought and died for the divinely constructed *eidôlon*, *gnômê* and "good counsel" (*euboulia*) make the best prophets (757); unlike Calchas's prophecy, *gnômê* does not depend for clarity upon the gods, who are regularly equivocal, or upon ambiguous mundane phenomena.[82] Theonoe, a priestess profession- ally intimate with *aithêr*, the "pure breath from heaven" (865–67), apparently exercises her *gnômê* when she decides not to denounce Helen: her perfect knowledge of every- thing divine and human remains equivocal because the gods themselves are divided, but Theonoe can resolve this difficulty by choosing actively what agrees best with her own nature (998f., 1002f.),[83] independently of what she knows, in a moral gesture equivalent to Aeschylus's artistic *authadeia*. With her ethereal *gnômê*, Theonoe decides to practice just deceit, which corrects the damage done by the ethereal *eidôlon*, the deceit of the gods.

Helen evidently exercises the same faculty with the same result, and so, at the end of the play, Theoclymenus congratulates her upon a "judgment most noble" (*eugenes- tatê gnômê*, 1687), which he says is found in many women, not one. But before Helen can use her *gnômê* and deceive Theoclymenus, she must first discover it, and her discov- ery marks the major turning point of the plot.[84] During its earlier phase, Helen has suffered passively from ap- pearances and from the confusions of *nous*: her beauty is a curse (261) and she sees herself as the work of some artist that had better be erased and made over (262–66); her reputation, as though personified, surrenders her to the lust of barbarians (224f.) so that men blame her for the be- havior of the *eidôlon*. As others believe the worst about her, Helen's own weakened spirit allows her to believe only the worst of what she hears about others. Thus, she imagines that Menelaus must be truly dead (279) because he is dead by reputation (132), and because the Dioscuri, her broth- ers, are "unseen" (*aphanes*, 207), she mourns them as if they were dead, although their disappearance merely pre- serves the equivocality of the two conflicting *logoi* about them (cf. 138). In her passive state, Helen chooses to be- lieve one *logos* and not the other without fully appreciating their equivocality and therefore without understanding that the choice offered by ambiguous appearances would allow her to believe the better rather than the worse.

When Helen exercises her *gnômê*, however, she has made herself the mistress of equivocality, and she uses it to deceive Theoclymenus, who believes what he wishes to believe without grasping his own part in the deception. Thus, she insinuates that she will be for him the sort of wife he deserves (1407) and that he will soon discover how much she loves him (1420); as the victim of this equivocality, Theoclymenus construes as true what seems "clear" to him (1200, 1202; cf. 308). The reversal in Helen's mental behavior is complete, for her insinuations play upon the appearances that tormented her before: she now asserts, without believing, that Menelaus is dead, and she surrenders herself, in speech, to "barbarian lust" (cf. 224f.); Menelaus's rags, which prevented her from recognizing him, lend plausibility to his newly assumed identity, and Helen's beauty, once a curse, now serves properly as a work of art (cf. 262) in a drama of feigned seduction.[85] Thus, Helen has made herself an *eidôlon* in Egypt, and, in her success as a deceiver, she earns the reward promised by the Dioscuri at the close of the play, to be a goddess, at least in name (1666–69), and so counted among the other cosmic causes of deception.

Here, then, is Euripides' elaboration of Gorgianic psychology: an active godlike power over appearances comes from the *gnômê*, an organ imbued with *aithêr*, the element in which the gods live and the medium of their art.[86] Among other masters of the *gnômê*, the poet may be singled out for special notice.[87] Like the Gorgianic audience of tragedy, Theoclymenus has become wiser for being deceived, and Helen has deceived her audience justly, like the Gorgianic poet. Her deceptions also connote the poet's work as Euripides represents it, for she uses the arts of Aphrodite, and Aphrodite appears in this play as a companion of the Muses and a mistress of healing song.

Before Helen sets about winning over Theoclymenus, she makes her peace with the goddess who had persecuted her, the mistress of "love affairs, deceptions, devious inventions" (1103f.). Aphrodite, says Helen, would be "the most delightful of gods" if only she were moderate (1105f.); now she too often causes bloodshed in the home. When Helen deceives Theoclymenus to save her husband, her virtue, and her marriage, she offers a paradigm of moderate life-preserving seduction, of Aphrodite's arts adapted to the service of domestic morality.

A different but consistent image of Aphrodite emerges in the ode to the Mountain Mother (1301–68), where she shares credit with the Muses and the Graces for diverting Deo from destroying the world. Salvation here depends explicitly upon the musical art over which these deities preside, and it is achieved by the means traditionally associated with poetry and the *logos*. Deo mourns the loss of her daughter with "unforgetting grief"[88] until her pain is stopped and she is made by choral songs to forget it (1344f.). This is the "forgetfulness of evils and rest from cares" that Hesiod identifies as the Muses' gift (*Th.* 55; cf. 102f.) and the charmed ease that song brings to Olympus in Pindar's first Pythian ode (1–12); it is associated by Gorgias with all forms of the *logos*, which can "take away pain (*lupê*) and implant joy" (*kharan*, *Helen* 8).[89]

If deception is defined in Gorgianic terms as something unreal rather than false, an experience made of words (or *aithêr*) that replaces physical sensation, the appeasement of Deo is a deception, and Aphrodite appropriately presides over it in her conventional role as a deceiver.[90] Euripides has altered the familiar Eleusinian myth, which makes Deo's appeasement depend upon Kore's release from the underworld for a part of each year.[91] In his own version, the world is saved before Deo finds what she seeks; the music that makes her smile takes the place normally occupied by her daughter.[92] Thus, music counterfeits a palpable satisfaction for Deo just as the *eidôlon* does for Paris and Menelaus.[93]

As the presiding deity in the Mother's musical appease-ment and in Theoclymenus's seduction, Aphrodite unites the poet's function with its conventionally negative count-erpart, sexual *parphasis*. The latter is Pandora's art, which is destructive because it deceives, according to Hesiod, and so distinct from benign (because truthful) poetry.[94] As Pin-dar represents it, poetry seems closer to seduction, but it must still be distinguished, as truthful and benign, from ruinous erotic deceit:[95] Aphrodite works in two ways (*N* 8), of which poetry aspires to imitate only one. In its moderate form as practiced by Helen, however, sexual deception ac-quires a positive value, and since Deo's cure is made to seem another sort of deception, poetry may now be identi-fied as Aphrodite's art without further qualification. Thus, Euripides explains Gorgianic *apatê* in mythic terms, by em-bracing in all its implications the affinity of poets to the goddess of sex.

ENCHANTING PRAISE: EURIPIDES
AND THE USES OF SONG

ᒪᒪᒪᒪᒪᒪᒪᒪᒪᒪᒪᒪᒪᒪᒪᒪᒪᒪᒪᒪᒪᒪᒪᒪᒪ

POETRY HAS TWO VIRTUES ACCORDING TO HOMER. IT is truthful and also pleasing, truthful in commemorating "famous deeds" and pleasing because it enchants: men are freed from self-consciousness, from the sense of present trials and personal need, as long as they hear the poet's song. Hesiod's poetry offers similar benefits, which he calls "memory" and "forgetfulness of cares." Pindar offers his audience a charm against anxiety, disappointment, and strife by truthfully displaying the splendor of human excellence. Apparently, then, the archaic poets describe their art according to a common pattern, endowed by Homer with the force of tradition. In this traditional pattern, the two virtues of song ideally coincide: song pleasantly enchants because it truthfully commemorates. Thus, poetry is a complex yet unified art, the art of pleasing truth, which is to say, of truthful enchantment.

There is an inherent tension, a source of instability, in this archaic program, however. Enchantment is a kind of diversion, which turns men away from their present condition, but the information that truthful song transmits is valued for its pertinence to present reality: as products of song, diversion and information seem to point in different directions. Therefore, as the archaic poets attempt to justify their art as consistent in its aims and effects, they must conceal, or else explain, an apparent anomaly.[1] In the Pindaric program, for example, it is praise that mediates and reconciles the tasks of diverting and informing an audience. Pindar's encomiastic poetry is diverting because the objects of praise are always splendid and exceptional, distant from ordinary, banal reality; it is informative and pertinent to the experience of its audience because it offers, with its timeless models of excellence, a practical guide to present conduct.

In Aristophanes' *Frogs*, however, the poets who compete for supremacy in the underworld speak for two distinct, apparently incompatible notions of poetic art. "Aeschylus" works the spells of enchantment, but these spells are now deceptive rather than truthful. "Euripides" offers a practical guide to conduct, but he has abandoned the task of praising excellence in favor of merely truthful description, the description of familiar, banal things; his poetry claims validity precisely to the extent that it is not enchanting. Thus, the model of a single art that offers enchanting, truthful praise has been purposefully abandoned, or else it has become unattainable.

The singers and consumers of song who appear in Euripidean drama also seem to envision two kinds of poetry, one devoted chiefly to enchantment, the other chiefly to a new, disenchanted sort of praise. Poetry traditionally achieves its double object by mediating between two conflicting motives—an unworldly desire to escape from the human condition and a worldly concern with the facts of human experience; in each of the new Euripidean poetic forms, one motive prevails over the other. Thus, enchanting poetry is defined in Euripidean drama by its unworldliness; it is prized or disparaged as an art opposed or irrelevant to mundane experience, an art that discounts, for better or worse, the reality of banal needs and banal satisfactions. Worldly motives, on the other hand, dominate the new poetry of praise. While the enchanted poet's morality requires a god as different as possible from human beings, for example, the encomiast's morality requires a god who is good in the same way that human beings are good, a god as much as possible like the encomiast himself, who will confirm his judgment and understand his need. Enchanting poetry makes men quiet and forgetful; the encomium makes them active and self-conscious. The new encomiastic poetry is prized for its utility, and it can be useful in two ways: as a truthful, morally valid account of human behavior and as an instrument of ambition, a source of strength and honor for the poet or the men he praises.

The validity of both poetic forms is a topic for debate in Euripidean drama. The poets and their audiences have become critics: the consumers of poetry argue with singers, and singers, in a private, reflexive way, struggle with their own uncertainty. It is this chapter's immediate purpose to clarify the issues and to identify the uncertainties in the Euripidean debate about song's validity. It is the chapter's thesis that the debate about song is generated by a single, fundamental problem, which Euripidean critics approach from different directions: when enchantment and praise are divided and their archaic unity is broken, the validity of both is diminished. The various sorts of dissatisfaction that Euripidean critics feel are symptoms of this loss, and they indicate that a valid art of poetry must offer truthful praise and enchantment combined. Euripides' own poetry seems to be such an art.

The aesthetic of enchanting poetry can be reconstructed from a group of fragmentary texts that have been associated, more or less certainly, with Euripides' lost *Antiope*.[2] Amphion, the play's protagonist, was traditionally identified as a poet, and Euripides has made him the type of the unworldly man,[3] appealing, it seems, to the notion that poets are typically quiet, contemplative, unworldly men. More specifically, Amphion seems devoted to the poetry of pure enchantment, a descendant of Homer's art that has been radically altered, with an escalating series of refinements, to suit post-Homeric sensibilities.

Amphion begins by excluding from his poetry "the city's ills" (fr. 202), the particular troubles presently faced by men around him. Evidently, he has applied a lesson taken from the eighth book of the *Odyssey*, where song enchants only those listeners to whom its subject matter bears no immediate relevance.[4] Next, following a more stringent aesthetic standard, Amphion shuns troublesome things categorically, for his art apparently ignores everything that is related to war,[5] and so it abandons Homer's effort to preserve for human audiences the memory of human trials suffered and overcome. Since the poet cannot commemorate the experience of men, he must turn, it seems, to the gods for his subject matter. Enchanting poetry offers its audience an illusion of sharing the god's felicity, and so with the Sirens' help (with song), men leave the world behind:

> I have golden wings upon my back,
> and the Sirens' winged sandals on my feet
> and I shall rise to the roof of aether
> to mingle with Zeus.[6]   (fr. 911)

A final refinement of poetry's subject matter makes the gods surrender their human qualities in obedience to the moral requirements of Xenophanes and Theagenes. When Xenophanes objected to Homer's stories of divine immorality,[7] Theagenes (and other allegorists of the sixth and fifth centuries) defended Homer by interpreting his gods as symbols for impersonal cosmological substances;[8] in the *Antiope*, apparently, anthropomorphic gods are replaced by Aether and Earth,[9] and so Theagenes' allegory becomes explicit. The enchanting vision that poetry now offers may be regarded as scientific and philosophical,[10] the "ageless order of immortal nature" (fr. 910)[11] that is purified of everything human, including the Homeric gods, whose happiness could be imagined as some perfect version of a man's.

These refinements of subject matter, which are designed to make poetry pleasing, are motivated by two assumptions. It is assumed first that the facts of human life are mixed, fortunate and also inevitably unfortunate (cf. fr. 196); thus, as a topic for song, human experience can never be made to seem simple or untroubled. It is also assumed that the poet's audience experiences directly what the poet

sings about. Thus, a song in which there remains any trace
of humanity cannot be pleasing because audiences will experience the song's description of the mixed condition of
other men as if it were their own.[12] Amphion seems to have
built his life entirely upon such principles. He believes that
he must free himself from contact with mundane things
in order to live pleasantly, for "things" are the cause of
human trouble: true prosperity, unmixed and independent
of changing fortune, is immaterial (fr. 198; cf. fr. 910).
Amphion also believes that it is possible to escape from
"things" because an experience of untainted, immaterial
prosperity—an experience as real for the spirit as the experience of things is real for the senses—can be created in
song. Song, then, becomes a place that Amphion can inhabit undisturbed, safely neglecting the palpable world (fr.
193; cf. frr. 187, 184).

The critics of enchanting poetry deny the possibility or
the value of an immaterial experience such as Amphion's
song promises, a spiritual life alternative to the life de-
pendent upon things. Because enchantment cannot provide this, according to one critical argument, it is useless
and provides nothing; according to another argument, enchantment can be pleasing, but pleasure does not justify
the poet's pursuit of enchantment. The nurse in Euripides'
Medea (190–203) denies that poetry provides any sort of
satisfaction that a feast does not also offer; thus, there is no
purpose in singing at a feast and no use for poetry when
real, material pleasures are available. On the other hand,
in the nurse's view, poetry cannot compensate for the loss
of such pleasures or cure men's pain; that is, it cannot enchant. Thus, since song's virtue does not differ from a
feast's and yet is nothing like a feast's, there is no utility at
all in song, and the "men of earlier times"[13] who brought
music to the feast were fools.[14] Amphion's brother Zethus
discovers a different sort of fault in the poet's pursuit of
enchantment, for he believes that enchantment distracts
men from something valuable in themselves. Pleasure, it

seems, is the only benefit that can be derived from enchanting poetry or from the purely contemplative spiritual life that enchantment makes possible. Because the souls of men possess a natural capacity for something more than pleasure, however, a man denies his nature when he devotes himself to song (frr. 186, 187). The enchanted life is a diminished life, and human nature can achieve its proper sort of excellence only in relation to the world of material things (cf. fr. 184). Thus, if poetry (or the poet's developed intellect) has any value in Zethus's view, it must contribute to the struggle with things: Amphion should sing about worldly human activities (fr. 188)[15] and so contrive some useful counsel for other men (fr. 185).

Zethus's program for song anticipates the arguments offered by "Euripides," the author of didactic, realistic poetry in Aristophanes' *Frogs*, and his quarrel with Amphion turns upon the same basic issues as the quarrel between "Euripides" and "Aeschylus."[16] For Zethus, the utility of poetry does not depend upon its enchanting power, the power to make a "place" furnished with immaterial objects so that an audience will respond to the poem as if to the experience of some palpable thing. Enchanting poetry promises an intrinsic benefit, the pleasure inherent in listening to song, and so enchanting poetry validates itself, if only as long as men remain enchanted. Worldly, realistic poetry, on the other hand, points beyond itself to the material world in which its audience lives, and so its validity is measured extrinsically, in the poem's clarity or truthfulness, and also in its practical utility, as a reflection of something else.

Worldly poetry is vulnerable to two kinds of criticism, which are inverted forms of the criticism applied to enchanting poetry. According to Medea's nurse, enchanting poetry fails in its own terms because it fails as a source of pleasure; according to the competing, worldly standard invoked by Zethus, it fails because it ignores the facts of human experience. Conversely, worldly poetry fails in its own terms when it is inaccurate or unclear as a reflection of the world; and, of course, it fails implicitly by Amphion's standard if it does not enchant. The chorus in the *Medea* seems to be concerned with the distortion of fact in worldly poetry and also with the perversion of enchantment as a condition of social life affecting poets and their audiences. The remedy it favors for these disparate problems seems to be the archaic art of enchanting, truthful praise.

The chorus complains that male poets have falsified their art to slander women and so to conceal their own misconduct; women have been unable to defend themselves because Apollo, the god "who initiates songs," has not allowed them the skill to sing (421–30). Thus, men have violated the worldly requirement that poetry should offer a truthful account of the facts, and they have also violated the special canons of encomiastic poetry by misrepresenting human vice and virtue. Since their art has become an instrument of ambition, the ambition to seem virtuous, their motive for spoiling song's validity as a reflection of the world has been worldly. Apparently, then, some kinds of poetic worldliness are self-defeating: song forfeits its claim to validity when it serves the narrow interest of person or faction.

Factiousness also troubles the chorus in the *Medea*. It is related to enchantment in some way, for it is a symptom of Aphrodite's influence upon the social relationships of human beings, and enchantment, by convention, is Aphrodite's function.[17] More specifically, according to the chorus, Aphrodite makes "temperaments disputatious and strife insatiable" when she is violent and excessive (627–41); she enchants when she is moderate, and her charms make men peaceful and honest. Men abide by their oaths, for example, when they feel a "spell"[18] cast by the sanctity of oath-taking; oaths have an attractive, compelling power (*kharis*, "grace," 439) that Aphrodite embodies more than any other goddess (cf. 631).[19] Thus, factious strife and enchantment are antithetical; they are also interchangeable because both are the work of Aphrodite, a goddess of double capacity.[20]

The chorus in the *Medea* wishes to be temperate (635), to be free of Medea's destructive fury, and so it wants an enchanting influence of the sort that Aphrodite in her moderate aspect provides. In the ideal society, as the chorus imagines it, poetry is the immediate source of this influence: at Athens, where Aphrodite is moderate (835–40), the Muses have given birth to Harmony (830–32),[21] a quiet condition antithetical to strife.[22] The food of the Athenians is *sophia*, the poet's art, as if they had made enchantment the stuff of daily life, and by this means, perhaps, they are enabled to breathe "most resplendent *aithêr*," the element of the gods.[23]

Thus, the chorus in the *Medea* wants truthful encomiastic poetry (an art that represents fairly the virtues and vices of men and women), and it wants enchanting poetry (an art that inspires honest, harmonious social behavior). Apparently, the chorus wants truthful, enchanting poetry, the archaic art, worldly and unworldly at the same time. Athenian society exhibits the double influence of this complex art, for it is active and successful by worldly standards as well as harmonious and quiet, sustained by the impalpable pleasures of song: Athens is a place where *areta* (excellent achievement) thrives (844f.). The Athenians, then, are not as enchanted as Amphion, whom Zethus charges with having neglected every kind of practical, manly virtue (frr. 184, 185, 187, 188), but they are enchanted enough to be peaceful, safe from "insatiable strife." In the *Medea*'s terms, poetry saves them from excessive *erôs*, an appetitive obsession with worldly, palpable things; in traditional terms, it makes them forget their quarrels and their cares.[24] The Athenians remain conscious of their material condition, however, and they continue to feel *erôs* in moderation, for their *areta* is the product of a collaboration between *erôs* (desire and worldly ambition) and *sophia* (the poet's art) (844f.).

Thus, at Athens the poets have discovered a middle ground in which the requirements of Amphion and Zethus can be reconciled, and this reconciliation is embodied in *areta*. Under the influence of his own enchanting poetry, Amphion does not pursue *areta*, apparently because he feels no worldly *erôs* and therefore sees no profit in struggling with material things; he claims only a quiet, inactive sort of virtue, which Pindar would call *aidôs*, restraint, and respect for gods and men.[25] At the other extreme of temperament, obsessive, appetitive men cannot achieve *areta* according to the chorus in the *Medea* (627–30). *Areta*, then, thrives only among men who have struck a balance between unworldly abstraction and worldly obsession; if poets foster *areta*, as they do at Athens, their songs must be balanced also.

Since the enchanting effect of Amphion's song seems to depend upon its unworldly subject matter, it is reasonable to suppose that the topics of balanced, worldly-unworldly songs must be mixed, or intermediate between Amphion's abstractions and the palpable objects of *erôs*. *Areta*, which Athenian poetry fosters, seems ideally suited to be the subject matter of a balanced art. It is a fact of human experience, inextricably rooted in the material world, and so it is an appropriate topic for poetry of the kind that Zethus wants, realistic and useful as a guide to conduct. (*Areta* is also, of course, the traditional concern of encomiastic poetry, and the validity of the encomium depends upon its truthfulness or fairness as an account of *areta*.) On the other hand, *areta* seems to be something more than a material, worldly thing because it is beyond the reach of men who are obsessed with palpable satisfactions (*Medea* 627–30). Thus, its nature is ambiguous, endowed with two kinds of reality. Pindar[26] suggests that *areta* is at once human and divine, ephemeral and eternal, a manifestation of "grace" from the gods in the world of things. For this reason, *areta* has a unique value for poets and for critics or consumers of poetry: a song that represents *areta* truthfully (an extrinsically valid, encomiastic song) should also be enchanting (an intrinsically valid, pleasing song).

Conversely, *areta*'s special quality as an enchanting, instructive topic of song makes it problematical, a touchstone of the poet's art and also of his temperament. Thus, the abstracted poet Amphion ignores the topic of human excellence and so displays an imbalance and a weakness of unworldly song; the factious male poets of the *Medea* give a false account of *areta* and so display an imbalance and a weakness of worldly song. Apparently, it is possible to devise a valid representation of *areta* (in a poem of enchanting praise) only if the poet has reconciled within himself the disparate impulses of worldliness and unworldliness.

The chorus of the *Heracles* professes its dedication to a balanced art, an art that derives validity as a source of pleasure and a medium of praise from its subject matter, the hero's *areta* (673–700). Ideally, according to this chorus (655–72), the encomiastic function normally associated with song might be otherwise performed if the gods were to reward *areta* by granting virtuous men a second youth: renewed youth would become a symbol of unmistakable clarity, and "by this means, it would be possible to tell the noble from the base" (665f.). Youth best qualifies for this symbolic use because it is also intrinsically desirable: as the negation of grim, hated old age (638f., cf. 649f.), youth is the remedy for "hateful pains" that Medea's nurse misses in song (195); since it is "always dear" and "finest in prosperity and in poverty" (637, 647f.), it meets her desire for something that will please men in difficulty as well as at ease.

Song is valuable to the extent that it serves as a substitute for youth: the old men of the chorus have aged irreversibly, but their grey beards do not diminish their paean to Heracles (691–94). Rather, their song defeats time and compensates for old age because it celebrates (and so preserves) Memory (*eti toi gerôn aoidos keladei Mnamosunan,*

678f.). In this way, like youth, it becomes a source of pleasure as well as a medium of praise. The chorus's song contrives the "sweetest joining" (675) between the Muses
(Memory's children, according to Hesiod), who may be regarded as patrons of the encomium, and the Graces, who
represent the song's pleasing,[27] enchanting[28] qualities. Heracles' *areta* is the unique and sufficient source, the material
cause, of this double validity in the chorus's song (680f.; cf.
659, 697 supp. Nauck).

Thus, the chorus in the *Heracles* describes its musical vocation according to a traditional scheme and also according
to the various requirements of the critics in Euripidean
drama, for its song of enchanting praise seems to embody
a compromise between the worldly and unworldly, extrinsic and intrinsic poetics of Zethus and Amphion. Since the
chorus defines its vocation as a response to *areta*, it confirms the *Medea*'s (and the tradition's) evidence of a natural
connection between *areta* and song.

Therefore, it is tempting to suppose that the old men of
the chorus speak for Euripides himself[29] or that the virtues
of their song directly represent the virtues of Euripidean
drama. This does not seem likely, however. The old men
are confused in their singing; they are uncertain of themselves and uncertain also of Heracles' *areta*, and their uncertainty points to the difference between an ideal type of
Euripidean poetry and their own version of enchanting
praise. Their vision is subtly distorted by worldliness, and
so their songs are deficient in enchantment and equivocal
in praise.

The old men value song to the extent that they value
Heracles' *areta*, but they also disparage song (and their
song is flawed) to the extent that they do not value or understand Heracles' *areta*. The chorus's regard for *areta* and
for song is changeable and contingent upon circumstance,
alternately faint and overconfident. When the hero is absent (and seems likely never to return), he is no longer
"great" (443f.); when he returns from Hades to save his

family, he is to be praised not merely as the son of Zeus but as something greater (696f.),[30] perhaps because he is more "present" than Zeus and serves his family's needs better.[31] As long as Heracles' strength and courage are visibly present to the chorus, the chorus seems to believe that the song of praise can be potent enough to replace the reward of redoubled youth: the song implicitly renews Heracles' *areta* by commemorating it, and it seems to renew the chorus's strength as well because the old men, once feeble, now feel inspired to dance like a band of Delian girls (685–94; cf. 107f.). On the other hand, when they believe that Heracles is dead, the old men feel no confidence in their singing; rather, song seems an old man's pastime, "words only and the fancy of nocturnal dreams" (*epea monon kai dokêma nukterôpon ennukhôn oneirôn*, 111f.).[32]

Apparently, then, the chorus has only a tenuous grasp upon the archaic program of enchanting praise,[33] and its doubts about song seem to originate in its sense of *areta* as a human, worldly thing. Pindar protects himself against such doubts with the notion that victory and good fortune, because they come from the gods, are more real than failure; thus, in Pindar's accounting, even the commemoration of victory, the reflection of past splendor as it is preserved in song, seems more real than present, actual "darkness" or pain. Pindar's song derives its power to enchant regardless of circumstance from the prepotent, divinely enhanced, unworldly reality of *areta*, its subject matter. Euripides' chorus, on the other hand, ascribes to Heracles' virtue a power that is purely human (because it does not come from Zeus), and this human virtue can be eclipsed by misfortune because it is no more real or memorable than any other fact of human experience. Thus, as a topic of song for Euripides' chorus, Heracles' virtue cannot wholly support the Pindaric program of enchanting praise.[34]

Conceived as a purely human phenomenon, Heracles' virtue might support another kind of enchanting praise, more secular than Pindar's odes: hypothetically, as the topic of Euripides' play, the hero's virtue endows Euripidean poetry with instructive, pleasing qualities. As Amphion suggests, however, the state of enchantment requires an unworldly (if not specifically divine) object of contemplation; therefore, human virtue must display some unworldly charm in order to make the poetry that commemorates it enchanting. As the chorus understands it, Heracles' virtue is a worldly thing, for it is defined chiefly by its palpable, present efficacy; conversely, Heracles cannot be "great" if he is dead. Thus, although the old men profess their dedication to the Graces' art, their song is not enchanting according to Amphion's standards.[35]

According to Amphion's standards, the *Hippolytus* comes to terms more adequately with the problematic of worldly and unworldly virtue; it also offers better models for a hypothetical Euripidean art of enchanting praise. Like Amphion, Hippolytus pursues the refined pleasures of an unworldly life, and his troubled confrontation with the world he wishes to shun suggests what difficulties an enchanted poet must encounter when he tries to adapt himself to mundane human expectations. Hippolytus's story is not, of course, an allegory for the poet's, but it exposes with unique clarity the charm of abstraction (which poetry evokes), and it displays the pattern of a reconciliation between abstraction and experience (which poetry ideally accomplishes). At the same time, the spectacle of Hippolytus's unworldly virtue made relevant to worldly life provides an exemplary topic for Euripides' own enchanting praise. This the playwright seems to acknowledge, for he presents Hippolytus explicitly as an object of awe persistently renewed in musical commemoration.

Hippolytus's qualities are defined partly by opposition. Phaedra's nurse, Hippolytus's antitype, is a disenchanted reader[36] of poetry and a determined pragmatist; like Zethus, she is contemptuous of unworldly pleasure that answers no present need. Her opinions are all modern. In her view, stories of the marvellous make no sense; they are irrelevant to the known conditions of life (*muthois d'allôs phe-romestha*, 197), like the story of Helen's birth condemned by the chorus of *Iphigenia at Aulis* (798–800). There is at least one awesome figure of legend who seems real and relevant to the nurse, however: Aphrodite is "more than a god" (359f.), an immanent fact of human experience (cf. 447f.). Thus, the nurse salvages practical knowledge from myth.[37] She believes that morality must be based upon need: virtue is less important than survival[38] or physical well-being, for with the first one wins only a "name" (*onoma*) or a "tale" (*logos*), with the second something real (*tourgon*, 501) and palpable (*ho anêr*, 491).[39] Such lessons can be learned and taught by people who read books: the nurse cites two groups as her authorities (451f), the poets and readers of poetry,[40] and she places herself among the learned, literary class, the few who know the legends of the gods.[41] These are the tools with which she undertakes her own sort of enchanting arguments (*logoi thelktêrioi*, 478), practiced first upon Phaedra and then upon Hippolytus. Her speech to Phaedra (451–78) is a reductive, inverted sort of praise: since poetry testifies that the gods are susceptible to love yet still inhabit Olympus, Phaedra's continued chastity would be presumptuous, her adultery venial (473–75).[42]

Temperament as much as dogma accounts for the nurse's modernism: she resists emotion that is too deeply felt, including her own sympathy for Phaedra (253–63), and, given the chance to collect her thoughts, she refuses to regard anything in this world as wonderful or mysterious (353–61; 433–38; 704f.). She clings to her sense of herself, to her sense of the present, even when this is painful, because, like Medea's nurse, she anticipates no "cessation of toils" (190), nothing in this life or the next (196) that brings relief. Therefore, she cannot understand Phaedra's yearning for "the absent thing" (*to apon*, 184f.), for rest in the distant meadow (*anapausaiman*, 211; cf. *anapausis*, 190) or a draught of pure spring water (208f.; cf. 225–27); similarly,

Medea's nurse ridicules escape from the "present thing" (*to paron*, 202f.) in song.

Phaedra's nurse, then, is a disenchanted reader of poetry because she is worldly in every other way, and what she does not understand or feel in her reading she misjudges in Phaedra and Hippolytus, their vision of some unworldly "absent thing" (184), "dearer than life" (191), and the *aidôs* it inspires. Both are drawn to the meadow in which Hippolytus worships his goddess. For Phaedra, it has a double charm: it is the place where her passion might be satisfied and also where her passion might harmlessly depart[43] if she shared Hippolytus's chaste pleasures, if she became manlike in the hunt, for example (215–22). Thus, in her delirium, Phaedra conjures up an equivocal fantasy, one aspect of which is worldly, inspired by an obsessive material need, for which untempered sexuality is the conventional paradigm, and the other unworldly, an enchantment that promises escape from need and forgetfulness of self. The first is vicious, and the nurse learns gradually to accept it; but the second is virtuous, it confuses her (cf. 236), and its final product, the suicide that erases Phaedra's passion and painful self-consciousness completely in favor of the thing literally "dearer than life," takes the nurse by surprise.[44]

For Hippolytus, the meadow's attraction is simple and unworldly: Aphrodite's charms do not enter there. It is irrigated by *aidôs*, the quiet virtue of Amphion. It is a place set apart, forbidden to ordinary men whose moderation (*sôphronein*, 80) is learned, not natural, so that the meadow is most particularly closed to people like Phaedra's nurse; the lessons she has drawn from mundane experience (252) or from the poets' tales of banal, erring gods (451–58)—her ways of withdrawing from pain and accommodating vice —do not apply there. As long as he remains in the meadow, Hippolytus need never learn the sort of moderation (*sôphronein*, 730f.) Phaedra wishes to teach him, the worldly virtue of yielding to circumstance.[45] The meadow is "untouched" (73) and, as the term is qualified elsewhere in the *Hippolytus*, this signifies two things: "untouched" by moral blemish, a quality that Theseus ironically ascribes to Hippolytus (949), and "untouched" by pain, a state to which the chorus aspires in prayer (1113f.). This double immunity is a privileged condition of gods so defined that they are as little as possible like men in character and experience; for Hippolytus, the essence of the difference is found in the purity of Artemis, a virgin beyond the range of the nurse's stories, whom he worships in the meadow on terms of special intimacy.

Hippolytus's intimacy with the goddess is limited, however, and its limits also define what the meadow offers: Artemis speaks to him but does not show herself (86); he has only *logoi* (85), nothing real or substantial, as the nurse would say (490f.). Thus, if Aphrodite is "more than a god" according to the nurse because her presence is universally manifest in the events of life, Artemis (or Artemis as Hippolytus knows her) might be called "merely a god" because she is less than present. Although the meadow provides physical props for physical activities—water for drinking, flowers for making garlands, wild animals to be hunted—its chief attraction consists in absence (its "untouched" purity) and near-absence (the spirit's experience of divinity made wholly from speech), something less than a life. As the chorus seems to suggest, this is all that the gods can normally offer men: spiritual experiences, conditions of the *phrenes*, that last only as long as inexperience of living. Purity is one (*ouketi gar katharan phren' ekhô ⟨ta⟩ par' elpida leussôn*, 1120 Hartung, Murray) and the comforting belief that gods care for men is another (*ê mega moi ta theôn meledêmath', hotan phrenas elthêi, lupas parairei*, 1104f.).[46]

The negative, chiefly spiritual blessings to be found in Hippolytus's meadow are characteristic of the class of such places and characteristic also of enchanting song. Thus, the meadow resembles the precinct in which Sappho imagines meeting Aphrodite (fr. 2 LP), an apple grove, shadowed with roses, where cold water flows (cf. *Hipp.* 208f.) and horses pasture (cf. *Hipp.* 230f.); she expects to be granted enchanted sleep there (*kôma*), a spiritual respite from passion and a feeling of divinely beguiled ease,[47] like the *kôma* induced by Apollo's music, which enchants the *phrenes* of Olympian gods (Pindar, *P* 1). Ibycus looks for a similar charm against the tempestuous *erôs* of his *phrenes* in an "untouched (*akêratos*) garden of the Maidens" (286 *PMG*). And it is reasonable to suppose that images of this kind provided the model for Pindar's description of paradise, a place of purified, musical delight for disembodied souls that was filled with horses and roses, and watered by smoothly flowing rivers,[48] and for Choerilus Samicus's description of the Muses' "untouched meadow" (*akêratos leimôn*, fr. 1 Kinkel).[49]

In none of these places, including the "place" evoked by song, may human beings remain and live; rather, their local qualities are like the songs enjoyed by audiences in the *Odyssey*, antithetical to the active experience of life, to appetite and effort, for the blessings they offer are negative, impalpable, and, except for the souls of dead men, necessarily intermittent. But for Hippolytus the meadow is a place to live, not an object of contemplation, the desired thing itself rather than its emblem; his devotion is active and unremitting.[50] In this respect he differs from other men, and the difference points to the play's major problem: the proper[51] relation between the meadow and daily life, between contemplation and conduct, enchantment and practical virtue,[52] *to apon* and *to paron*.

Hippolytus's virtue is tested, when he faces first the nurse and then his father, by the need to assess judiciously the impurity he encounters in the world and to communicate the authenticity of his own pious, unworldly condition to an audience ignorant of the meadow. His task is encomiastic and rhetorical, like Pindar's, and he must choose, as Pindar chooses, between speech and silence about crime. If he accuses Phaedra, he breaks an oath of secrecy (656–58) and offends the gods (cf. 1033); he might also diminish his own purity because the words condemning Phaedra would carry the taint of the deeds they picture. (He must wash his ears when he has heard the nurse's proposition because in the realm of the spirit where Hippolytus lives, even representations of sexuality are dangerous and offensive.)[53] On the other hand, if he does not speak or speaks ineffectively, Hippolytus confirms his father's delusion and forfeits his honor.

With doubly fatal effect, Hippolytus vacillates between the two extremes avoided by Pindar.[54] His disgust at the revelation of Phaedra's weakness makes him furiously denounce all women (616–50),[55] and his blaming speech elicits from Phaedra a vengeful, defensive accusation in return. With Theseus, Hippolytus remains inhibited and ineffective in representing his own virtue. Piety makes him suppress the truth about Phaedra, and something similar apparently frustrates his attempt to tell the truth about himself. He is, he says, not "musical" when speaking to the crowd but "wiser" or better skilled in the company of a few young men (986–89); nevertheless, he must speak to Theseus (990f): Theseus is the "crowd." More precisely, Theseus makes Hippolytus feel less than eloquent because he does not belong to the select group intimate with the meadow, whose virtue is natural, not learned (79f.); he belongs (with Phaedra's nurse) to a worldly audience that knows only what it learns and learns only from mundane experience or perhaps from reading. Thus, Theseus cannot recognize what devotion to the meadow entails, and because such virtue is exceptional, Hippolytus cannot prove that it is real: all young men are lustful, and therefore, Theseus reasons, Hippolytus must be too (966–70).

Hippolytus's failure confirms his belief that teaching is vain (cf. 921f.), and so, it seems, he forfeits his life to the exclusive principle, speaking, like Pindar, only to the wise (O 2.83–85). But with his unskillful "music," he has failed in the poet's first task: because he does not communicate his unworldly virtue, he does not enchant; he is a "charmer" and a "wizard" according to Theseus (1038), but his charms are ineffective, as the result indicates. Disenchanted and unenlightened, Theseus commits the crimes that he ascribes to Hippolytus: he violates the sanctity of their kinship[56] and disregards the sanctity of Hippolytus's oath (cf. 1320–22, 1307–9).

When Hippolytus has been mortally injured, however, this pattern reverses itself: Theseus learns *aidôs* (1258f.) as if death has begun to make Hippolytus's virtue palpable to worldly senses even before Artemis arrives to proclaim it *ex machina*; Hippolytus learns to pity Phaedra and Theseus,[57] and Artemis retreats from his suffering, leaving him nothing but human affinity and worldly experience.[58] The compensation Hippolytus receives for his suffering (1423) reflects this late reconciliation between unworldly virtue and worldly experience. As he lies dying in his father's arms, Artemis promises him a cult in which virgin brides shall sing his story forever and make him offerings of their hair (1423–30). The honor seems unsuitable judged by the meadow's standard, for it celebrates (as it mourns) virginity's loss in conjunction with Hippolytus's death. But the cult provides what Hippolytus could not give Theseus, a musical (1428f.) expression of the "absent thing" Hippolytus cherished and a fair, explicit judgment of the "present thing" he shunned: it preserves at least a memory of purity, encapsulated in ritual within the context of normal sexual life, and grafted upon this enchanting vision, in place of Hippolytus's silence (1430), it offers the story of Phaedra, made harmlessly into praise.

By entering in this qualified way into the desire for enchantment, the cult defines a middle ground where ritual, like art, attenuates human suffering without effacing it and where divine felicity is made visible and pertinent to human aspiration. There is a psychic geography implicit here in which the emotional claims of present and absent things are balanced,[59] and its landmarks have been figuratively defined by the chorus. In their imagination, the women fly from the familiar and the real, from Phaedra's trouble, over the Adriatic to the edge of the world and the boundary of heaven (732–51). Human beings cannot reach this place by physical means (744f.); it contains inhuman objects of enchanted contemplation, Zeus's marriage bed and the song of divine singers. But there is an intermediate stage in their journey that retains a memory of suffering and transforms it into something immortal and fine: by the fabulous river Eridanos, Phaethon's sisters forever weep "amber beams" of tears (737–41), mourning their mortal brother who, like Hippolytus, tried and failed to live with the gods.[60] Grief thus purified and distanced would offer the chorus an accessible refuge, and it signifies the best that art may accomplish while still remaining in contact with the conditions of human life—the distance of enchantment and the nearness of remembering praise. Perhaps, then, the image may serve as a model for understanding the poetics of Euripides' tragic play.[61]

THE APPARENT CONTRADICTIONS OF EURIPIDEAN
and Aristophanic poetry arise from the poets' attempt to
reconcile the complex demands of traditional poetics in a
coherent form. By the end of the fifth century, this tradition has become unstable: Euripides and Aristophanes discover an unresolved dialectic in the program that seemed
to satisfy their predecessors; they depict the emergence of
new kinds of poetry—distorted fragments of an older,
more comprehensive art—which are justified or criticized
according to equally new, polemical standards of judgment. Both of them evidently wish to reassemble these
fragments, to recapture the balance and the integrity of the
archaic art. Aristophanes looks for a synthesis of "Euripidean" clarity and exemplary, "Aeschylean" virtue; Euripides, who sees the problem differently, offers a synthesis in which poetry becomes half-abstracted from the
mixed, imperfect excellence of men. At the same time,
both poets remain sensitive to the contradictions inherent
in their archaizing programs, and their self-conscious, di-
alectical response to their predicament marks the last stage
of an obsolescent tradition.

The fifth-century predicament can be explained as the
result of a major dislocation in the history of Greek poetics.
It occurs at the end of the archaic period, when Homer's
account of poetry has been altered in two ways. There has
been a change in the perceived status of poetry as a source
of useful knowledge, as an art pertinent to the mundane
activity or experience of its audience, and a change also in
the definition of enchantment, the audience's experience of
poetry itself and its immediate response to the singer's
performance.

In Homer's view, the singer's truthfulness seems to be
guaranteed by his distance from his audience: he is a professional, a specialist in singing, who shares none of his lis-

teners' ordinary concerns; he performs as much for the gods who provide his skill as for human beings who provide his sustenance, and his divine patrons make him independent of any human influence that might diminish his song's validity. Thus, the bard can sing "as his own mind urges," and although he normally pleases his audience in this way, he need not consider the pleasure of his audience when he chooses the "path" of his song. As Homer indicates, most listeners allow this latitude to poets because they do not expect to discover in song anything that touches directly upon their own experience or desires; song's undiminished truthfulness is simply a source of pleasure, something to be valued without reference to the mundane context of performance. A single bard, practicing his art consistently according to the single standard of accuracy, can please the suitors and Odysseus, Odysseus and the gods.

Homeric song, then, cannot be useful in an ordinary way because its validity depends upon its unworldliness. For Odysseus, however, the song of Demodocus is valuable because it recalls the hero to himself and so lends significance to his present endeavors; thus, Odysseus differs from other members of the poet's audience. Odysseus is also depicted as a peculiar sort of singer, a storyteller who uses the singer's art deceitfully, for amusement (to tantalize his friends) and for gain (to confound his enemies). Homer does not explain the significance of this worldly, quasi-poetic art, but it clearly differs in a fundamental way from the old unworldly, truthful song.

Odysseus the storyteller no longer seems abnormal when he is judged by Hesiod's standards or by Pindar's. Hesiod can imagine a deceitful poet—his Muses tell lies. Pindar knows that there are malignant poets—Archilochus, for example (*P* 2.55f.). In the context of Pindaric poetry, Odysseus's behavior as an audience also seems normal, for Pindar's patron expects to find his achievement reflected in song. The poet's account of past events illuminates the present, and it offers a useful guide to successful, virtuous activity in the future.

Thus, the poets who follow Homer narrow the distance between the poetic art and other human activities, between poets and other men. Homer's influence works obliquely, for Hesiod and Pindar seem more concerned with the problem of Odysseus, an exception to the most ancient Homeric rules, than with Demodocus or Phemius, in whom these rules are exemplified.

A more radical deviation from the Homeric model can be observed in the developing notion of enchantment, the audience's experience of song in performance. According to Homer, the singer pleases his listeners because he diverts them from self-consciousness; as long as they listen to song, they seem to inhabit a world other than their own, a world in which they can remain disengaged, untroubled observers. Their experience of song resembles an experience of the underworld, which Homer depicts as a place without physical or emotional substance: in the underworld, one perceives the truth of things, but one cannot feel any palpable sort of reality. Because the experience of song differs in this respect from the experience of life, even grim and fearsome things evoked in song can pleasantly divert an audience.

Hesiod seems to offer another sort of benefit to his audience. The truth he promises is more restricted than Homer's "orderly" truth: Hesiod will uncover something visible only to divine insight. With song's divine insight, for example, men can remember their original condition of perfect felicity, a condition that the gods have since reserved exclusively for themselves; with song's help, men can even "remember" the future. Like Homer, Hesiod promises to divert his audience, but the diversion of Hesiodic poetry is pleasing not because poetry evokes an attenuated, impalpable, untroubled experience of troublesome things but rather because it evokes a vision intrinsically superior to mundane, human experience.

Pindar's notion of enchantment differs most radically from Homer's. For Pindar, speech possesses the moral quality of the things it represents so that the reality of things is not attenuated in poetry. (Speech about crime, for example, is criminal speech; crime does not become ghost-like and untroublesome when poets commemorate it.) Therefore, Pindar must be selective in his choice of subject matter; his poetry obscures the painful or criminal aspects of human experience, but it preserves a special, restricted "truth," the memory of triumphant virtue. This, Pindar suggests, is a divine sort of truth, like Hesiod's, a god's vision of history in which only god-given "grace" seems real. Poetry makes this vision vivid and "present" to its audience because speech embodies the reality of whatever it commemorates. (Specifically, in Pindar's poetry, virtuous speech embodies "grace.") This is how Pindaric poetry enchants: as the past, the present, and the future seem equally vivid to the gods, the poet's account of past and future events can seem as real to his audience as the circumstances of performance. Pindaric enchantment brings a selective but not a distanced vision of things.

Thus, Pindar's art differs from the Homeric singer's in two ways: Pindaric poetry speaks directly to the listener's present concerns, enhancing his self-consciousness, and it offers an enchanting experience that seems as immediate and real as the experience of daily life; Homeric poetry subverts the listener's self-consciousness, and it offers a different sort of enchantment, an attenuation of experience, ghostlike and unreal. Pindar's novel aesthetic requires a novel justification, the principle of moral selection. According to this principle, poetry inspires a beneficent, useful sort of self-consciousness because it makes the listener conscious specifically of his virtue; the immediacy of the poet's language, its power to embody as a present thing the crime or virtue in distant events, is controlled by the same rule of selection. The justification of Pindaric poetry depends also, of course, upon the notion that a partial vision of things can be valid: for Pindar, it is validated by the gods.

The language of Aeschylus, like Pindar's language, embodies whatever it describes; Aeschylean enchantment creates a vivid, magically real experience for the audience. But Aeschylus seems to reject Pindar's partial vision and the theology upon which it depends. Rather, he suggests, the divine vision is complex, the complex vision is valid, and so the complexity of human experience is irreducible in poetry: virtuous and criminal deeds equally require commemoration, for example. It is clear, therefore, that Aeschylean poetry cannot be useful or beneficent in the same way as Pindar's because its indiscriminate, complex vision imposes a fearsome experience of moral confusion upon the audience; clarity and justice, if they can be achieved at all, must be earned by the audience, as a reward, it seems, for having suffered at the poet's hand. In this respect, the experience of poetry seems to offer no advantage over the experience of life.

As if the example of Aeschylean enchantment overtaxed the fifth century's theoretical resources, subsequent programs for poetry are more circumscribed and less problematical. The poets who imitate Pindar's morally selective, partial vision, having lost their divine warranty, no longer claim to be truthful; rather, they suggest that a beneficent, morally valid art of enchantment must be deceptive—the more vivid the enchantment and the more effective the poet's moral influence, the more skillfully deceptive the poet must be. These poets share Pindar's belief that the use of language entails a moral choice, that language has a kind of reality or moral "weight," but they define this choice in purely subjective terms. Thus, although the poet does not report god's truth, he can invent his own, a truth he chooses, in a godlike act of creation. Gorgianic artists— "just deceivers" like Aristophanes' Aeschylus and Euripides' Helen—practice this new creative art.

For another kind of artist in the fifth century, language does not possess "weight." It is an empty, morally neutral medium of description, a collection of signs that merely refer to things and do not embody them. Poetry therefore does not exert a moral influence, and it does not enchant its audience. Apparently, it does not evoke even an attenuated experience of things, a diverting, Homeric kind of enchantment, for the audience must remain sober and self-conscious to interpret the signs of speech. Thus, in contemporary terms, Euripides' distanced, Homeric enchantment represents a compromise between the vivid "presence" of Gorgianic speech and a competing ideal of disenchantment, between the chosen, morally appropriate or pleasing "truth" and pragmatic realism. For disenchanted, sober audiences, there is nothing more at stake in poetic speech than clarity or accuracy; poetry can be useful, but it is useful only as an instrument, subordinated to the pursuit of real benefits in the context of daily life. Otherwise, the disenchanted complain, it is "only words."

In retrospect, then, one observes a rising ambition among poets of the archaic period, an ambition to evoke the vision of gods, to work more potent forms of enchantment, and to contribute more directly to the conduct of active, daily life. With Pindar, this development seems complete, until it is carried forward, and confounded, by Aeschylus, a sophisticated artist who works in the powerful, apparently inexplicable, medium of primitive word-magic. The circumscribed and diverse accounts of poetic art that emerge later in the fifth century may be regarded as fragments of the developed archaic program.

ᒪᒪᒪᒪᒪᒪ ABBREVIATIONS ᒪᒪᒪᒪᒪᒪ

AJP	*American Journal of Philology*
CP	*Classical Philology*
CQ	*Classical Quarterly*
CR	*Classical Review*
DK[8]	*Die Fragmente der Vorsokratiker,* ed. Hermann Diels and Walther Kranz, 8th ed. (Berlin, 1956)
HSCP	*Harvard Studies in Classical Philology*
JHI	*Journal of the History of Ideas*
JHS	*Journal of Hellenic Studies*
Mnem	*Mnemosyne*
N[2]	*Tragicorum Graecorum Fragmenta,* ed. August Nauck, 2d ed. (Leipzig, 1889)
NGG	*Nachrichten von der Gesellschaft der Wissenschaft zu Göttingen*
NLH	*New Literary History*
PCPS	*Proceedings of the Cambridge Philological Society*
PMG	*Poetae Melici Graeci,* ed. Denys Page (Oxford, 1962)
RhM	*Rheinisches Museum*
TAPA	*Transactions of the American Philological Association*
YCS	*Yale Classical Studies*

CHAPTER ONE

1. *Od.* 8.536–43, 581–86.

2. For the connection between the passages, see G. N. Knauer, *Die Aeneis und Homer* (Göttingen, 1964), index at 376.

3. Walter Marg, *Homer über die Dichtung*, 2d ed. (Münster, 1971) 20, would make the Phaeacians atypical here. Cf. J. M. Redfield, "The Making of the Odyssey," in *Parnassus Revisited*, ed. Anthony Yu (Chicago, 1973) 151, who makes a similar choice between Telemachus and Penelope, preferring the engaged to the disengaged audience.

4. Cf. Herwig Maehler, *Die Auffassung des Dichterberufs im frühen Griechentum bis zur Zeit Pindars*, Hypomnemata 3 (Göttingen, 1963) 33.

5. Cf. the use of *epistasthai* for knowledge of fact (*Od.* 4.730) and for manual dexterity (21.405f., *Il.* 5.60f.).

6. For the lies of Odysseus, see the last section of this chapter.

7. Odysseus's account of the good speaker differs from Alcinoos's of the singer in one respect. Alcinoos infers truth from verbal *morphê*, whereas Odysseus discovers a social virtue in the speaker's words. The singer must have knowledge and be willing to share it; the speaker must have *aidôs* (172), regard for his listeners. The speaker's intellect corresponds to the singer's knowledge, the social "grace" of speech to song's truthfulness, but in either case verbal *morphê* follows automatically from the first two conditions.

8. Cf. *ou kosmôi* of disordered retreat on the battlefield (*Il.* 12.225); for the expression *eu kata kosmon*, cf. *Il.* 10.472, 11.48 = 12.85; *Hom. h. Hermes* 475ff. *kosmos* seems to denote a verbal order, metrically defined, in Solon 1.2 West.

9. Cf. G. S. Kirk, *Heraclitus: The Cosmic Fragments* (Cambridge, 1954) 312, especially on the "semi-logical" use of *kosmos*, and passages cited there.

10. This is T. B. L. Webster's interpretation of the passage, "Greek Theories of Art and Literature down to 400 B.C.," *CQ* 33 (1939) 175. Cf. Hans Diller, "Der vorphilosophische Gebrauch von ΚΟΣΜΟΣ und ΚΟΣΜΕΙΝ," in *Festschrift Bruno Snell* (Munich, 1956) 57, who compares *Od.* 14.363. For another view, see Tilman Krischer, "ΕΤΥΜΟΣ und ΑΛΗΘΗΣ," *Philologus* 109 (1965) 171.

11. For the moral significance of *kosmos*, cf. Solon 7.11 West, cited by Diller (above, n. 10) 55. A set of rules, specifically artistic, governing the composition of song could conceivably emanate from society, as Marg suggests (above, n. 3) 19: "Die Sang folgt festen Regeln, ist kunst-

gerecht"; for the wider application of *kata kosmon*, cf. A. W. H. Adkins, "Truth, ΚΟΣΜΟΣ, and ΑΠΕΤΗ in the Homeric Poems," *CQ* 22 (1972) 5–18.

12. Cf. Diller (above, n. 10) 57: "Aber die Wahrheit erscheint als 'Ordnung,' entsprechend der epischen Auffassung von der richtige Sprache, die Wort am Wort reiht."

13. Cf. Adkins (above, n. 11) 14.

14. For occupational skill derived from the gods, cf. *Od.* 7.110, 19.396; *Il.* 13.730 (*polemêia erga*). For the completion of an action given by the gods, cf., e.g., *Il.* 14.86.

15. *oimai* is generally taken as "paths of song" or narrative lines, stories. Cf. W. B. Stanford, *The Odyssey of Homer*, 2d ed., rev. (London, 1964) ad *Od.* 22.347 and Rosemary Harriott, *Poetry and Criticism before Plato* (London, 1969) 65.

16. Homer seems to distinguish song from its subject matter once, with the adjective *aoidimos*, "subject of song" (*Il.* 6.358); or does this mean "worthy of becoming an *aoidê*"?

17. See *Il.* 2.484–86; cf. *Od.* 12.189f. For a different account of knowledge, the Muses, and the poet's craft, see Penelope Murray, "Poetic Inspiration in Early Greece," *JHS* 101 (1981) 87–100.

18. Cf. Joseph Russo and Bennett Simon, "Homeric Psychology and the Oral Epic Tradition," *JHI* 29 (1968) 483–98 and Albin Lesky, *Göttliche und menschliche Motivation im homerischen Epos* (Heidelberg, 1961).

19. Cf. the account of "theme" given by Gregory Nagy, "Formula and Meter," in *Oral Literature and the Formula*, ed. B. A. Stolz and R. S. Shannon (Ann Arbor, 1976) 247.

20. What we would call "distortion" would be inevitable, of course, but oral poets do not seem to worry about preserving stories with verbatim accuracy; see Albert B. Lord, *The Singer of Tales*, paper ed. (New York, 1965) 99–123. Regarded as the actions narrated, the song of Achilles, for example, will always be the same: cf. Nagy (above, n. 19) 277.

21. Thus, according to Lord (above, n. 20) 13, "composition and performance are two aspects of the same moment."

22. For Telemachus, however, novelty is not inevitable: some songs are more novel, and therefore more popular, than others (1.351f.). Since the song is identified by its subject matter, what men want, according to Telemachus, is a new, unfamiliar story; the *Odyssey* is an old story for Homer's contemporary listeners (they know at least that the war at Troy was finished long before their time), and so Telemachus's statement represents what Homer might regard as an ancient as opposed to contemporary attitude. The conceit, Homer's attempt to show that the old epic stories once were young, seems to indicate a view of poetry fundamentally at odds with Phemius's and Alcinoos's assumptions, a conscious-

ness of tradition and of distance from the immediate, divinely preserved truth; as a case in point, the verisimilitude of this scene is obviously manufactured. For other departures from the view of Phemius and Alcinoos, see comments on Odysseus later in this chapter. For a very different interpretation of Telemachus's statement, see Giuliana Lanata, *Poetica pre-platonica* (Florence, 1963) 19.

23. The medium for the Homeric poet is specifically the dactylic language with its formulae or formular patterns.

24. E. N. Tigerstedt, "*Furor Poeticus*: Poetic Inspiration in Greek Literature before Democritus and Plato," *JHI* 31 (1970) 168, resolves the apparent contradiction in Phemius's statement by asserting that *autodidaktos* is the same as *theodidaktos*; E. R. Dodds, *The Greeks and the Irrational* (Berkeley, 1951; paper ed., 1963) 10, believes that to a Homeric audience the two claims will not seem contradictory because they imply the same thing, that Phemius has not been taught by other minstrels. See also W. K. C. Guthrie, *A History of Greek Philosophy* (Cambridge, 1962) 1:415; Harriott (above, n. 15) 95; and Walther Kranz, "Sphragis," *RhM* 104 (1961) 4.

25. For an "unforgetting" truth (*a-lêtheia*), see Marcel Detienne, *Les maîtres de vérité dans la Grèce archaïque* (Paris, 1967) 24–27. For another notion of truth (and another interpretation of *alêtheia*), see chapter 2; cf. Detienne, 48 n. 107.

26. See above, n. 17.

27. For a traditional audience, then, a song fashioned according to traditional rules is all surface, like the *Odyssey* itself as Erich Auerbach described it in *Mimesis*, trans. W. R. Trask (Princeton, 1953; paper ed., 1968) 3–23.

28. Thus, he would not be "following a story," as W. B. Gallie describes the process, in *Philosophy and the Historical Understanding*, 2d ed. (New York, 1969) 22–50.

29. His experience of song is like a god's, as Phemius seems to suggest (22.348f.), and this makes sense because the singer's knowledge is a god's (cf. *Il.* 2.484–86).

30. Cf. *Hom. h. Apollo* 161.

31. Cf. also 10.291, 326; 5.47; 24.3.

32. This is joined with the human action of *parphasis*, performed *malakois epeessi* (16.286f.; cf. 19.5f.). For *parphasis* as a function of speech related to poetry, cf. chapter 2 on Hes. *Th.* 79–90 and chapter 3 on Pindar *N* 8.

33. The closely bound roles of Memory and Forgetfulness in Hesiod's account of the effects of poetry (*Th.* 54f.) and the affinities of song to death and the underworld in the *Odyssey* complement certain religious and philosophical doctrines of a later date linking Memory and Forgetfulness to the underworld. See J. P. Vernant, "Aspects mythiques de la

mémoire et du temps," in *Mythe et pensée chez les grecs* (Paris, 1965) 59, e.g. Entering the realm of the dead, one forgets one's past and personal experience, just as the singer's audience forgets itself in the enchantment of song and learns instead something timeless and divine; cf. "Orpheus" fr. 17 DK[8].

34. In this way, Phemius is distinguished from the seer, whom Odysseus suspects of having prayed for the suitors' advantage. The singer, by contrast, is supposed to be untouched by worldliness and therefore immune to corrupting influence. In fact, as Jesper Svenbro argues, Homeric singers were sensitive by necessity to the beliefs and the desires of their listeners; see *La parole et le marbre* (Lund, 1976), especially 16–35. In a fluid, oral tradition, however, the singer need never acknowledge this fact, even to himself: he need not see that he sings differently at each performance (since he does not attempt to imitate exactly some original version of the song); that is, he need not see that he may have introduced a particular fact or point of view or moral value into the story he tells; therefore, he need not see that he might do this to please his listeners. Penelope questions the singer's choice of subject matter, and Alcinoos asks Demodocus to stop singing, but neither expects to change the song itself; for traditional audiences, the singer remains essentially beyond influence. Only Odysseus, a novel kind of listener at odds with the tradition, intervenes in the singer's making of the song.

35. Cf. Achilles, *Il.* 9.189; in the *Odyssey*, however, singers are always professional.

36. 1.369f. The formality of the performance varies among oral cultures: see Dennis Tedlock, "Toward an Oral Poetics," *NLH* 8 (1977) 515, on the difference in this between Zunis and Maya. In the *Odyssey*, storytelling is less formalized than singing (cf. 4.238f.).

37. It is perhaps the singer's unworldliness that makes him an appropriate watchman of Clytemnestra's virtue (3.265–72).

38. Pindar works a different sort of enchantment from a different sort of truth: see chapter 3.

39. It does not follow that Demodocus cannot sing *kata kosmon* if he sings *kata moiran*: the *kosmos* perhaps consists of *moirai* properly measured and marked, and so Odysseus might find the emphasis he wants in a song that traditional listeners perceive as "orderly" (but he would not necessarily find it there).

40. The process is associated especially with speech that leads (or is meant to lead) to action—warnings (15.27), advice (18.129), or plotting (16.259)—and with speech that provokes an immediate emotional response, for example, the various stories about Odysseus's return told to Penelope (17.153, 19.268) and Laertes (24.265); cf. 20.92 (Odysseus's response to Penelope's lament), and *Il.* 19.84 (the response Agamemnon wants when he apologizes to Achilles).

41. This is the interpretation of Stanford (above, n. 15) ad loc.

42. If Helen's story presents a typical incident, perhaps its content is *eoikota* in a second sense, "probable things."

43. In this respect, Helen's story, and any poem fashioned like Helen's story, would differ from the *Odyssey* as Auerbach describes it (above, n. 27).

44. Telemachus is the only exception to this rule: he wants to hear Phemius's song because it especially concerns him as the son of Odysseus (μελήσει . . . μάλιστα δ' ἐμοί, 1.358f.), but he seems entirely unmoved by it. His response betrays his youth and his inexperience; when he comes later to the palace of Menelaus, he weeps more readily (4.113–16, 150–54, 184f.), as his father weeps among the Phaeacians. On Telemachus's immaturity as an audience, see Redfield (above, n. 3) 152.

45. For the relative dates of the two passages, see chapter 2, n. 13.

46. Apparently, Odysseus's lies enchant Eumaeus (17.521).

CHAPTER TWO

1. For pleasure (*terpein*), see *Od.* 17.385, 1.347, 8.45, 8.368, 12.188; for beguilement (*thelgein*), 1.337, 12.40, 44, 17.514, 521, 11.333 = 13.1, and *Hom. h. Apollo* 161.

2. For destructive enchantment, see *Od.* 16.297f., e.g.

3. Cf. Alcinoos's praise of Odysseus, *Od.* 11.363–68.

4. The word is not Homeric: cf. M. L. West, ed., *Hesiod Theogony* (Oxford, 1966; repr. 1971) ad loc.

5. Since Hesiod's song concerns the future as well as the past (*Th.* 32), memory must take both as its object, an anomaly one might explain in two ways: the future will replicate or reflect the past because Hesiod sings of the gods "who are forever" (105); or, "memory" need not exclusively denote recollection. For the latter, cf. Alcman 118 and 133 *PMG*.

6. Cf. "Musaeus" fr. 7 DK[8].

7. Cf. Athanasios Kambylis, *Die Dichterweihe und ihre Symbolik* (Heidelberg, 1965) 61, who identifies *kalê aoidê* (*Th.* 22) with truth.

8. Cf. West (above, n. 4) 184 ad 84ff.

9. Nothing, that is, unless Apollo as the god of prophecy is taken to signify song's truth here. It is impossible, however, to discover whether this is what Hesiod meant, or whether poetry and prophecy would seem to him related arts. L. R. Farnell's evidence in *The Cults of the Greek States* (Oxford, 1907) 4:245 and n. 2, postdates Plato.

10. What men do not know without song is precisely what Zeus intends for them: cf. *WD* 483f.

11. For *homoios* as "like" linking two things that are in some respect

significantly different, cf. *Il.* 5.778f. and 10.437; *homoios* also seems
to signify "identical" or "same" in some Homeric passages (cf. R. J.
Cunliffe, *A Lexicon of the Homeric Dialect*, s.v.), but it cannot do so at *Th.*
27. If *pseudea* are "identical" to *etuma*, they will differ not at all from
alêthea (28).

12. For *etumos* as "true," cf. *muthos etêtumos*, *Od.* 23.62; "real" ("possible"), cf. *nostos etêtumos*, *Od.* 3.241. I do not wish to make distinctions
where the Greek has none, but it would perhaps be proper to say that
etumos and its cognates cover a range of meanings within which any
particular usage requires narrower definition. Here, as at many other
points in my argument, I find myself crossing ground recently covered
by Pietro Pucci, *Hesiod and the Language of Poetry* (Baltimore and London,
1977). I agree with Professor Pucci too often and have profited too much
from his book to acknowledge each of his prior claims in these notes.

13. Cf. *Od.* 19.203. I follow Friedrich Solmsen, "The 'Gift' of Speech in
Homer and Hesiod," *TAPA* 85 (1954) 10-13, in taking the Homeric passage as earlier; cf. West (above, n. 4) 184 ad 84ff. For Odysseus as a
singer, cf. *Od.* 11.367-69, 17.518-21. See also Heinz Neitzel, "Zum
zeitlichen Verhältnis von Theogonie (80-93) und Odysee (8,166-177),"
Philologus 121 (1977) 24-44.

14. The listener's disbelief in the true elements of Odysseus's stories
suggests the complexity of the expression "lies like facts" as the starting
point for a theory of rhetoric. For Eumaeus, see *Od.* 14.360ff.; Penelope,
19.260-307, 19.583, 20.232.

15. E.g., *Od.* 18.366-86.

16. 82 B11 DK[8], 15-18.

17. Plato objects (*Rep.* 606d) to what Gorgias celebrates: the poet's and
the painter's images arouse the emotions just as the conduct of life does
(ἃ δή φαμεν πάσῃ πράξει ἡμῖν ἕπεσθαι), by appealing to the irrational
part of the soul. This kind of success is not attempted by the Homeric
artist, however. Achilles' shield, covered by pictures made by
Hephaestus's divine skill, does not terrify the Achaeans (19.14f.) because
they mistake these pictures for reality and respond with emotions appropriate to what these pictures represent; they are terrified by the
shield's evidently unearthly provenance. Its worked gold "looks like"
(*eôikei*, 18.548f.) black plowed earth, but this merely makes the shield an
object of wonder (*thauma*) and calls attention to the artisan's skill. (For
the translation "looks like," cf. T. B. L. Webster's different interpretation,
"Greek Theories of Art and Literature down to 400 B.C.," *CQ* 33 [1939]
177 n. 14; for the perception of skill in realistic representation, cf. Aesch.
fr. 17.7 [Mette], where graphic accuracy reveals the maker's hand [τὸ
Δαιδάλου μ(ε) [ί] μημα, 7]. The satyrs here are somewhat more sophisticated than "the savage gaping at the wonders of photography," for the
savage does not compliment the photographer; see G. F. Else, " 'Imita-

tion' in the Fifth Century," *CP* 53 [1958] 78.) When graphic or vocal mim-
icry arouses emotions in the audience (cf., e.g., *Od*. 4.278–83), it does so
by means not apparently available to epic poetry. When Hesiod's Muses
mimic the real by singing *pseudea etumoisin homoia*, they must dissemble
their skill to command belief, but they do not therefore seek to elicit
emotion.

18. This, and what follows, alters the emphasis placed by Wilhelm
Luther, "Wahrheit, Licht und Erkenntnis in der Philosophie bis Demo-
krit," *Archiv für Begriffsgeschichte* 10 (1966) 42–44, upon the worldliness of
Hesiod's poetry.

19. For the poet's independence of experience, cf. *WD* 660–62.

20. For justice as a result of forgetfulness, see *WD* 263f.

21. Cf. *Lexicon des frühgriechischen Epos*, s.v. ἀληθείη, and Paul
Friedländer, *Plato*, trans. Hans Meyerhoff, 2d ed. (Princeton, 1969)
221–29.

22. Cf. Luther (above, n. 18) 36ff. He denies that a distinction should
be made between *alêtheia* as a quality of things and of speech, because
"die Dinge und die sie bezeichnenden Wörter noch in einem untrenn-
baren Wirkungszusammenhang stehen" (37).

23. This is possible and desirable because listeners like Alcinoos infer
truth from verbal form (*Od*. 11.363ff.).

24. Cf. *Od*. 24.200 for Clytemnestra as *aoidê*.

25. Cf. Albert B. Lord, *The Singer of Tales*, paper ed. (New York, 1965)
28f., on the singer's view of verbal invariance.

26. Cf. *Il*. 2.485f. One might also say that song is *kleos* of a superior
sort because it is transmitted only once, from the gods who are eyewit-
nesses to everything that has happened.

27. Thus, Hesiod occupies a position between the Homeric singer,
who denotes what he knows by naming his subject (above, n. 24), and
Solon, who distinguishes his art by its words (*kosmon epeôn*, 1.2 West); at
13.52 *metron* could refer to the metrical patterns of poetry (cf. Plato, *Lys*.
205a, where *metra* are "verses"), or merely a measured "amount" (cf.
Theognis 876).

28. Hesiod will anticipate Theognis, if one believes that Theognis, by
naming himself, sets a "seal" (*sphrêgis*) upon his work against the danger of interpolation or corruption (19–23). See, e.g., Albin Lesky, *A History of Greek Literature*, trans. James Willis and Cornelis de Heer, 2d ed.
(New York, 1966) 170 and Richard Reitzenstein, *Epigramm und Skolion*
(Giessen, 1893) 265, who translates Theognis 21 as "niemand wird sie
ändernd schlechter machen wollen"; against this reading, cf. Leonard
Woodbury, "The Seal of Theognis," *Phoenix* supp. 1 (1952), who denies
that Theognis was concerned with other poets' "tampering" with his
work (23, 28, 30), and M. L. West, *Studies in Greek Elegy and Iambus*
(Berlin and New York, 1974), who, like Woodbury, separates the "seal"

from 21f. and paraphrases "no one will substitute a bad (author's name) when the good is at hand. Everyone will identify Theognis of Megara" (149).

29. She is not their mother in the *Iliad* and the *Odyssey*; cf. Alcman 8.9 *PMG*; Solon 13.1f. West; and the explicitly literate concern of Aesch. *PB* 789, 460f. West (ad *Th.* 54) may be correct to say that "the importance of memory to the oral poet needs no stressing," but it is noteworthy that the Homeric singer does not consider memory worth mentioning because he relies entirely upon the knowledge of the gods, whereas Hesiod, less certainly an oral poet and less sure of his Muses, does.

30. Cf. West ad 233.

31. On the relation of poet and audience, cf. Marcel Detienne, *Les maîtres de vérité dans la grèce archaïque* (Paris, 1967) 69: "Ce qui est mémoire pour le poète est oubli pour autrui."

32. Cf. the very different argument of Pucci (above, n. 12) 24.

33. Cf. 235f. (*oude themistôn/ lêthetai*) and West (above, n. 4) ad loc.

34. Despite *Th.* 591ff and *WD* 373–75, some women in this world must be good and not all need be like Pandora, as the expression *aidoiê parthenos* suggests; if Pandora mimics only one sort of girl, she can represent only one sort of art. For the sense of *aidoiê*, cf. *Il.* 21.460; *Hom. h. Apollo.* 148; Hes. *Sc.* 14, 46; *Th.* 953.

35. Pindar corrects this asymmetry in *P* 1, representing Zeus's eagle as soothed into sleep by Apollo's lyre.

36. Hesiod's Muses seem to have omitted the present from their song intentionally. Cf. *Th.* 32 and the Homeric prophet Calchas, who knows τά τ᾽ ἐόντα τά τ᾽ ἐσσόμενα πρό τ᾽ ἐόντα (*Il.* 1.70).

CHAPTER THREE

1. Pindar distinguishes himself in this way from Phemius and from Homeric singers generally. Cf. *Od.* 22.344–52 for the singer's art as a benefit to be judged without reference to social conditions: Phemius sings to the gods, and he bears no responsibility for the crimes of the suitors, his human audience.

2. See above, chapters 1 and 2: among audiences of song, Homer's Odysseus and Hesiod's Zeus are significant exceptions to this rule.

3. *Od.* 1.56; *WD* 78.

4. Cf. *O* 8.54.

5. It is not clear in this context whether the "invisible" is something unreal or something ignominious: see below on *Nemea* 5.

6. For the complexity of deceit, cf. Pindar's use of *poikilos*, *O* 1.29; *N* 5.28f; for truthful simplicity, see chapter 4, n. 1.

7. The inherent "light" of real achievement shines unsteadily because

human fortune changes and men are a "shadow's dream" (*P* 8.88–97), essentially dark and insubstantial even at the peak of success; cf. *N* 7.12f. for the "darkness" of valor in the absence of song. For *P* 8, see Hermann Fränkel, "Man's 'Ephemeros' Nature According to Pindar and Others," *TAPA* 77 (1946) 131–45, especially 131–34.

8. It is symptomatic of this difference that *parphasis* kills Ajax, but Pindar's poetry cannot bring the dead to life (*N* 8.44f.).

9. Cf. *N* 7.14. "Reflection" is the least that poetry offers.

10. Cf. fr. 106b Bowra = 121 Sn-M; *O* 2.46f.; *P* 5.103f. (*prepei*). Also cf. *eoiken*, fr. 234 Bowra = 42 Sn-M; *O* 1.35; *potiphoros*, *N* 3.31; *N* 7.63.

11. For the use of silence, cf. Simonides 582 *PMG*; Pindar fr. 170 Bowra = 180 Sn-M; Hermann Gundert, *Pindar und sein Dichterberuf* (Frankfurt, 1935) 47.

12. For the nature of the "profit" named here, see below, n. 54.

13. Cf. the "hateful song" of Clytemnestra, *Od.* 24.199f. For the senses of Pindar's phrase, see LSJ, s.v. μέγας, II.5. L. G. Dissen, *Pindari Carmina*, vol. 2 (Leipzig, 1830) 415, followed by Johann Rumpel, *Lexicon Pindaricum* (Leipzig, 1883; repr. Hildesheim, 1961) s.v., renders μέγα as *audax, malum*. Cf. J. B. Bury, ed., *The Nemean Odes of Pindar* (London, 1890; repr. Amsterdam, 1965) ad loc. and W. J. Slater, *Lexicon to Pindar* (Berlin, 1967) s.v.; see also *N* 10.64. For μέγα εἰπεῖν used positively ("to say something great"), cf. *N* 6.27.

14. Cf. fr. 234 Bowra = 42 Sn-M; inappropriate silence makes valor dark, *N* 7.12f.

15. Cf. *N* 7.61 (undeserved reproach). The punished criminal is metaphorically "dark," Aesch. *Ag.* 390–93; cf. 462–67.

16. *N* 1.8–12; cf. *O* 6.8, 11f.; *O* 8.67–69. For silence, cf. fr. 70 Bowra = 81 (*Dith.* 2) Sn-M.

17. Cf. *P* 9.76–79.

18. Cf. Solon 13.65f West; see below, nn. 82 and 83.

19. For the quality of Pindar's "inspiration," see the final section of this chapter.

20. ἐπεὶ ψεύδεσί οἱ ποτανῷ ⟨τε⟩ μαχανᾷ / σεμνὸν ἔπεστί τι.

21. ἐμᾷ ποτανὸν ἀμφὶ μαχανᾷ.

22. Cf. fr. 98 Bowra = 108 Sn-M; cf. "the pure road of god-given deeds" (*I* 5.23) and Otfrid Becker, *Das Bild des Weges und verwandte Vorstellungen im frühgriechischen Denken*, Hermes Einzelschriften 4 (Berlin, 1937) 61.

23. Cf. *N* 2.7 and Becker (above, n. 22) 65. The formula for prayers called hypomnesis is based upon this tendency for events to proceed in a "straight" line as they have begun: cf. *P* 1.46; *O* 13.28.

24. *O* 13.13: ἄμαχον δὲ κρύψαι τὸ συγγενὲς ἦθος.

25. This statement, or others like it, may have discomfited Pindar's competitors. According to the scholiast, it answered Simonides 602

PMG; cf. Bacchylides fr. 4 Jebb. Cf. *N* 1.33–34b; *I* 4.21–25; *I* 1.39f. for the antiquity of virtue.

26. The expression (διορθῶσαι λόγον) is ambiguous: B. L. Gildersleeve, *Pindar: The Olympian and Pythian Odes* (New York, 1890; repr. Amsterdam, 1965) ad loc., paraphrases διελθεῖν ὀρθῶς; it is thus unclear whether the story is constructed by Pindar or merely followed by him. For another view of the sense of *orthos*, see D. C. Young, *Three Odes of Pindar* (Leiden, 1968) 78 n. 2; for *orthos* as "straight," cf. *O* 7.46; *P* 11.38f. Becker (above, n. 22) 72 sees the path of *P* 11 as an image for the "program" of Pindar's poem rather than the course of the historical narrative.

27. *Sophia*, of course, also entails other qualities: cf. Bruno Snell, *Die Ausdrücke für den Begriff des Wissens in der vorplatonischen Philosophie* (Berlin, 1924) 1–20, especially 10–13; G. F. Gianotti, *Per una poetica pindarica* (Turin, 1975) 95–107; Burkhard Gladigow, *Sophia und Kosmos* (Hildesheim, 1965) 39–55.

28. Cf. *O* 10.53–55; for this process as the result of god's intervention, cf. *N* 7.31f.

29. Cf. *Paean* 6.51–53 and Gladigow (above, n. 27) 43.

30. By contrast, with better than human vision, the god who perceives what is hidden in the future (*horan*, 62; *kekruphthai*, 57) keeps to the proper course: Helios forbids a backward turn (ἄμπαλον . . . θέμεν, 61), and he commands Lachesis not to deflect or perjure the gods' oath (θεῶν . . . ὅρκον μέγαν/ μὴ παρφάμεν, 65f.). Helios's straight action, sight, and speech are set against the mistakes of deviation (*parelkei, pareplanxan, parphamen*).

31. Cf. *O* 13.10: "Bold-speaking" Hubris provokes Koros in its audience. Thus, it is significant that Pindar inverts the relationship between Koros and Hubris (cf. Solon 6.3 West, Theognis 153): Hubris, for Pindar, must be the mother of Koros rather than her daughter because *hubris* (which speaks excessively) belongs to the (bad) poet and *koros* is the effect of his poem; cf. *P* 8.29–32.

32. There seems to be a similar process at work in the behavior of heroes who feel "regard" (*aidesthentes*) for their own valor (*P* 4.173).

33. Thus, Pindar inverts the Hesiodic paradox (*Th.* 54f.) that Memory bore the Muses who bring forgetfulness.

34. For this process, cf. P. Laín Entralgo, *The Therapy of the Word in Classical Antiquity* (New Haven, 1970) chaps. 1 and 2, especially 45–52.

35. See above, chapter 1.

36. Cf. *O* 2.15–20; *O* 6.103f.; *O* 8.72–74; *N* 10.24 for the comfort that victory and good fortune bring.

37. Cf. 67–72 and Young (above, n. 26) 93 n. 2.

38. An elaborate hypomnesis comprising the entire description of the erupting volcano is concluded at 29ff. with an invocation to Zeus. The story of Philoctetes, who suffered and triumphed, makes for hypo-

mnesis by analogy, concluding with a prayer (56f.) for Hieron's success (and, implicitly, for the cure of his disease).

39. See also 34–38.

40. For Apollo's music and Pindar's, cf. *elelizomena* (4) ~ *doneôn* (44); *balein* (44) ~ *ambolas* (4).

41. *Kêla*: perhaps, as the scholiast sensed, this is a pun on *kêlein*.

42. See above, chapter 1.

43. For a musical *boa*, cf. *O* 3.8; *P* 10.39; *N* 5.38, each cited by Gildersleeve (above, n. 26) ad loc.

44. *Il.* 6.41; 21.4, 554; cf. *Od.* 11.606.

45. Elsewhere, they are terrified (*atuzomenoi*, 8.183), in contrast to the Trojans, whom Hector exhorts to remember their courage (μνήσασθε δὲ θούριδος ἀλκῆς, 174; cf. 181, μνημοσύνη τις ἔπειτα πυρὸς δηίοιο γενέσθω).

46. See above, chapters 1 and 2. Homer's Sirens kill their audiences, of course, but Homer does not seem to regard this fact as problematical for the human singer's art; Hesiod's Muses presumably work harm when they deceive, but Hesiod would distinguish such deceit from his own poetry.

47. Cf. the two kinds of "peace," *P* 8.1–20.

48. For other affinities between the two passages, cf. S. D. Skulsky, "ΠΟΛΛΩΝ ΠΕΙΡΑΤΑ ΣΥΝΤΑΝΥΣΑΙΣ: Language and Meaning in *Pythian* 1," *CP* 70 (1975) 9–12.

49. Two things keep Typho in his place: the Muses' shout inspires terror, and he is "confined" beneath Aetna (κίων δ᾽ οὐρανία συνέχει, 19b) just as the eagle is "possessed" (κατασχόμενος, 10) by the lyre's sounds. Music and the mountain seem to serve the same purpose. The monster does not sleep because the rocks that contain him, like the shout that astounds him, also keep him in pain (27f.). For wakefulness as part of the punishment of confinement, cf. Aesch. *PB* 31f.; for Prometheus and Typho, see J. P. Vernant, "Mètis et les mythes de souveraineté," *Revue de l'histoire des religions* 180 (1971) 29–76, especially 61–63.

50. As the obverse of the poet's praise for his patron, these sounds resemble "hateful speech" (*ekhthra phatis*, 96) that "possesses" (*katekhei*; cf. *kataskhomenos*, 10) evil Phalaris like a charm, as if he still lived and listened in dismay to what men say of him; the *ekhthra phatis*, however, is not musical.

51. Cf. M. R. Lefkowitz, *The Victory Ode: An Introduction* (Park Ridge, N.J., 1976) 110f. on the volcano and the song as a coordinated antithesis.

52. Cf. Solon fr. 1 West for poetry as an alternative to (*anti*) public speech.

53. *Od.* 22.344–52: see above, n. 1.

54. For diplomatic silence in Homer, cf. *Il.* 10.533ff. and *Od.* 4.138ff., which are cited and discussed by A. W. H. Adkins, "Truth, ΚΟΣΜΟΣ,

and ΑΠΕΤΗ in the Homeric Poems," *CQ* 22 (1972) 14. The social benefits of silence may be identified, perhaps, with the *kerdos* named in *N* 5
(16f.).

55. See, e.g., *P* 10.66, for the poet and patron as bound by the loyalty
of *philoi*. For other relationships, see Gundert (above, n. 11) 31-39.

56. Cf. W. J. Verdenius, *Pindar's Seventh Olympian Ode: A Commentary*,
Mededelingen der koninklijke nederlandse Akademie van Wetenschap-
pen, Afdeling Letterkunde, n.s. 35 no. 2 (Amsterdam, 1972) 4, for the
problems of interpreting this passage.

57. *P* 2.96; *O* 1.115b-116; for the sense of *agathos* in this context, see
R. W. B. Burton, *Pindar's Pythian Odes* (Oxford, 1962) 87 on *P* 3.80-83.
Pindar acknowledges a positive obligation to the *agathoi* with whom he
associates: for the rules of behavior associated with *kharis*, see Gianotti
(above, n. 27) 19-28; Gundert (above, n. 11) 31-39, 42-45; Herwig
Maehler, *Die Auffassung des Dichterberufs im frühen Griechentum bis zur Zeit
Pindars*, Hypomnemata 3 (Göttingen, 1963) 86-88; J. W. Hewitt, "The
Terminology of 'Gratitude' in Greek," *CP* 22 (1927) 151-53.

58. For the Danaans' "service" as *parphasis*, compare the prize they
offer (*antetatai*, 25) with *kudos* that *parphasis* gives (*anteinei*, 34b). For the
flattery implicit in this service, cf. Bury (above, n. 13) ad loc., but it is no
more than an implication; *therapeuein* is explicitly deceptive in Thuc.
3.12.1.

59. *kruphiaisi . . . en psaphois*, 26; for the ominous connotation of secrecy, cf. *N* 9.33, *O* 1.47.

60. For the affinity of deceit and violence, cf. Hes. *Th.* 226-29.

61. *Hôra potnia*. But the relative clause (2f.) makes better sense as a
description of Aphrodite herself. Cf. C. Carey, "Pindar's Eighth Nemean
Ode," *PCPS*, n.s. 22 (1976) 27.

62. Cf., e.g., Hippolyta in *Nemea* 5 (29-32); *Il.* 14.214-17. Cf. also Pandora's *haimulioi logoi*, *WD* 78.

63. In the Homeric poems, poetry and sex are both sources of enchantment, but the charm of sex is normally baneful and the charm of
poetry benign. (Cf. Aegisthus's seduction of Clytemnestra, *Od.* 3.264,
and the suitors' infatuation for Penelope, 18.212; for the singer, cf.
17.514-21.) Thus, in making poetry sexual in its charm, Pindar conflates
two distinct Homeric categories, but he has distinguished constructive
from destructive "erotic" relationships so that *parphasis* alone and not
poetry will bear the opprobrium of seduction and deception.

64. "Among" = ἐν supp. Boeckh. For *ebrise* (18) and fertility, see Bury
(above, n. 13). For the two kinds of *erôs*, one of them an incentive to
areta, cf. Euripides in Hans von Arnim, *Supplementum Euripideum* (Bonn,
1913) 44, lines 29-32; for a literal explanation of the association between
erôs and excellence, cf. Plato *Symp.* 178a6-180b8.

65. For the *kairos* as a "right time" for *erôs*, cf. frr. 108 Bowra = 123 Sn-M, 112 Bowra = 127 Sn-M.

66. Cf. the desire for gain as a cause of "deviation," *P* 3.54f.

67. Cf. *P* 2.34; *I* 6.71.

68. For *aidôs* as a check upon desire, cf. the association of *aidôs* and *kerdos* in Theognis 83–86 and Pindar *N* 9.32–34, as cited by C. E. von Erffa, *AIΔΩΣ und verwandte Begriffe in ihrer Entwicklung von Homer bis Demokrit, Philologus* supp. 30/2 (Leipzig, 1937) 71, 76.

69. For *aidôs* and excellence, see Erffa (above, n. 68) 77 and *O* 6.76. Cf. n. 76 below.

70. See Erffa (above, n. 68) 82f. on piety.

71. For the "restrained" disposition and social harmony, cf. S. Eitrem, "The Pindaric Phthonos," in *Studies Presented to David M. Robinson*, ed. G. E. Mylonas and Doris Raymond, vol. 2 (St. Louis, 1953) 534, on the opposition of *harmonian blepein* (*P* 8.68) and *phthonera blepein* (*N* 4.39).

72. For the connotations of *allotriôn*, see the schema of Young (above, n. 26) 116.

73. Cf. *O* 1.46–53. For abuse of the gods as a symptom of *mania*, unmeasured desire, cf. *O* 9.37–39.

74. It inhibits him from commemorating crime, *N* 5.14.

75. For the sense of the passage, see Gildersleeve (above, n. 26) ad loc.

76. Cf. *O* 7.88f.; also see *O* 13.115f., where Pindar prays that his patrons win *aidôs*.

77. *P* 1.86f.; cf. *N* 8.20–22, part of an elaborate justification for offering praise despite the danger of provoking *phthonos*. For blame as the outcome of success, see *O* 6.74f.

78. The bridle with which Bellerophon controls Pegasus is called both a *philtron* (*O* 13.68; cf. 85) and a *metron* (20).

79. On the connection between these passages, see Burton (above, n. 57) 92.

80. If Fränkel (above, n. 7) has correctly rendered the sense of *ephameros* as connoting a mental sort of variability that makes men think vain and "childish" thoughts (cf. fr. 143 Bowra = 157 Sn-M) and so rebel against divine dispensation (cf. *P* 3.82 and the child's pleasure disparaged by Pindar, *P* 2.72f.), then the timeless historical perspective that Pindar offers in *Pythia* 1 may be regarded as another inducement to moderation: seeing permanent, god-given benefits, the audience that Pindar has instructed should also learn to accept passing frustrations with pious equanimity. But cf. Matthew Dickie, "On the Meaning of ἐφήμερος," *Illinois Classical Studies* 1 (1976) 7–14, especially 8f. on *P* 8.95.

81. *O* 2.86; *O* 9.28f.; *P* 1.41f.; *O* 11.10.

82. fr. 50 Bowra = 61 Sn-M.

83. Cf. *N* 6.6–7; *N* 11.43f.; *O* 12.7–12.

84. *Sophia*, therefore, is dangerous and ambivalent; if it is not always controlled by piety, it can be used destructively (cf. *N* 7.23). Perhaps in this sense *sophiai* are also "steep" (*O* 9.107f.; cf. *N* 5.32b for the meaning of *aipeinos*).

85. Cf. *Paean* 6.5f., however, where Pindar claims to act as the Muses' "spokesman" (*prophatas*).

86. For Pindar's sobriety, cf. Giovanni Brancato, *Quattro note di filologia classica* (Messina and Florence, 1960) 60; for the question of inspiration in general, E. N. Tigerstedt, "*Furor Poeticus*: Poetic Inspiration in Greek Literature before Democritus and Plato," *JHI* 31 (1970) 163–78, especially 173–75 on Pindar as *prophatas* and *mantis*. For *mania*, cf. *O* 9.37–39 and Plato *Phdr.* 245a.

87. "Invention" in another context (*O* 13.17; cf. 74) means finding what the gods give. Also, see above, n. 26, on *O* 7.21.

88. According to this rationale, piety is inspired by the old lesson that gods give men two portions of trouble for every "noble" benefit: see *P* 3.80–83.

89. Cf. fr. 234 Bowra = 42 Sn-M and Burton (above, n. 57) 87.

CHAPTER FOUR

1. See George Thomson, ed., *The Prometheus Bound* (Cambridge, 1932) 137, citing Aesch. fr. 176 N² = 288 Mette, Eur. *Phoen.* 469, Ar. *Plut.* 1158; cf. Pindar *N* 8.32–36 (κελεύϑοις ἁπλόαις ζωᾶς).

2. *O* 1.28–29; cf. *N* 5.28–29; *O* 7.53.

3. For the positive sense of *poikilos*, cf. *N* 8.15; *N* 5.42b; *O* 6.85–87; *O* 3.8–9.

4. For "high" or "elevated" style as a product of nature or inspiration, cf. Fritz Wehrli, "Der erhabene und der schlichte Stil in der poetisch-rhetorischen Theorie der Antike," *Phyllobolia für Peter von der Mühll* (Basel, 1946) 23–33.

5. *O* 2.83–86.

6. There are more metaphors in the *Agamemnon* than in any other extant Aeschylean play, fewer in the *Eumenides* than in any except the *Persians*; see F. R. Earp, *The Style of Aeschylus* (Cambridge, 1948) 97. On the assumption that Earp's criteria for identifying metaphors are consistently applied, his relative measurements may be regarded as valid.

7. For the meaning of this passage, see Eduard Fraenkel, ed., *Aeschylus: Agamemnon* (Oxford, 1950; repr. 1962) 3 : 575f. ad *Ag.* 1244. For the topic of obscurity and "interpretation," cf. *Ag.* 615f., 1062f., 1162.

8. On the meaning of *etumos* and the problem of identifying Aeschylean etymologies, see Anne Lebeck, *The Oresteia: A Study in Language and*

Structure (Washington, D.C., 1971) 213 n. 5. For examples, see Walther Kranz, *Stasimon* (Berlin, 1933) 287–89; Fraenkel (above, n. 7) ad *Ag.* 682.

9. For the significance of *autodidaktos*, see above, chapter 1.

10. εὔχομαι δ' ἐξ ἐμᾶς / ἐλπίδος ψύθη πεσεῖν / ἐς τὸ μὴ τελεσφόρον.

11. See H. D. Cameron, "The Power of Words in the *Seven Against Thebes*," *TAPA* 101 (1970) 95–118; J. J. Peradotto, "Cledonomancy in the *Oresteia*," *AJP* 90 (1969) 1–21; Ernst Neustadt, "Wort und Geschehen in Aischylos' Agamemnon," *Hermes* 64 (1929) 243–65. For the problem of interpretation posed by magical speech, cf. *PB* 486f.

12. Cassandra's reply, that nothing will "heal" what she has said, indicates how closely word and event are bound together; see Neustadt (above, n. 11) 251, and cf. *Ag.* 498f.

13. Later, another chorus prays for the accomplishment of evil speech as vengeance in return for evil speech (*Ch.* 309): ἀντὶ μὲν ἐχθρᾶς γλώσσης ἐχθρὰ/ γλῶσσα τελείσθω.

14. Cf. Neustadt (above, n. 11) 256–61.

15. Cf. ἀπέρωτος ἔρως, the corrected (and possibly accurate) manuscript reading at *Ch.* 600, printed by A. W. Verrall, *The 'Choephori' of Aeschylus* (London and New York, 1893), and by Gilbert Murray in his Oxford text of the play (Oxford, 1955), but rejected by George Thomson in *The Oresteia of Aeschylus* (Cambridge, 1938).

16. See the discussion of *nomos anomos* later in this chapter.

17. For the shared concerns of Heraclitus and Aeschylus, see Wolfgang Rösler, *Reflexe vorsokratischen Denkens bei Aischylos* (Meisenheim am Glan, 1970) 4–6, 12–15, especially 14 n. 35 on the topic of etymology. There is no need, of course, to posit Heraclitus's direct influence upon Aeschylus.

18. Zeus's perplexing mutability corresponds, perhaps, to the danger presented by equivocality in language: cf. *WD* 483f.

19. See above, chapter 2: since Hesiod wishes to forfeit neither of these virtues, he must claim privileged status for his own poetry, at least implicitly, and to guarantee his own truthfulness, he must offer a proof extrinsic to the poetry itself.

20. Or, Heraclitus assumes the complex validity of speech and wishes to demonstrate that death and life are the same: cf. G. S. Kirk, *Heraclitus: The Cosmic Fragments* (Cambridge, 1954) 118.

21. Fr. 93: it is hard to imagine why Heraclitus should comment upon Apollo's oracle except as an illustration of some general truth; in any case, if language possesses natural validity independently of the speaker's knowledge, no use of language (including the god's) should differ essentially from any other.

22. For the difference between "signifying" and "speaking," cf. *Ag.* 494–98.

23. Cf. frr. 54, 51, 123.

24. Thus, the chorus seems to mean that a funeral rite performed for Agamemnon by Clytemnestra should not be regarded as *kharis* (1543–46).

25. For *logos* as "word," see Kirk (above, n. 20) 39. For the position of Heraclitus with respect to parataxis in archaic thought, see A. P. D. Mourelatos, "Heraclitus, Parmenides, and the Naive Metaphysic of Things," in *Exegesis and Argument*, ed. E. N. Lee, A. P. D. Mourelatos, and R. M. Rorty, *Phronesis* supp. vol. 1 (Assen, 1973) 32f.

26. *Akharis kharis* possesses a similar double sort of complexity, which the characters of the *Agamemnon* implicitly simplify in two forbidden ways, by limiting the sense of each word and by eliminating one of the two words from their interpretation of the figure. When the chorus describes the funeral rite (1545), it denotes Clytemnestra's role as a grieving wife with the term "grace" and her behavior as Agamemnon's killer as "graceless"; "graceless grace" suggests the conflict between these two roles. Clytemnestra, however, would reverse the sense of each word: she possesses the right to bury Agamemnon—and so to act with "grace"—as his killer, not his wife (1551–53); if there is anything "graceless" in the funeral, on the other hand, it must be the presumption of a widow's grief (cf. 1554). Thus, there are two definitions (murder and marriage) for both terms of the figure and two ways of simplifying each term, each dictated by the interpreter's moral perspective. The chorus also seems to imply that Agamemnon's funeral will not be a "grace" in any sense (and that the figure has a literal sense, "graceless"); the two roles cannot overlap and the two terms denoting these roles cannot be meaningfully combined because Clytemnestra as killer has replaced Clytemnestra as wife. Clytemnestra herself insists that she is not to be called Agamemnon's wife (1498f.) and therefore that the two roles do not overlap; but she would interpret the literal sense of "graceless grace" as "grace." Thus, the chorus's negative moral judgment discounts the positive term, and Clytemnestra's positive moral judgment discounts the negative. Both interpretations of the figure are partial, and the moral problem is reflected in the complexity of the language.

27. For an account of this process, see chapter 5.

28. Although there must be, in fact, an elaborate, unconscious mental process behind any "automatic" apprehension of meaning, this phenomenon need not be acknowledged by a magical theory of speech: cf. chapter 5 for the emergence of self-conscious linguistic analysis. For the emphasis placed upon the result of a mental process rather than upon the process itself, cf. Kurt von Fritz, "ΝΟΟΣ and NOEIN in the Homeric Poems," *CP* 38 (1943) 89f.

29. For resistance and submission to fate as it is given in names, cf. Cameron (above, n. 11) 107–9, 118. For Agamemnon's yoke, see n. 56 below.

30. Agamemnon attempts to defend himself from the unwanted linguistic sign of kinship by suppressing Iphigenia's inauspicious cries (*klê-donas*) of "Father" (*Ag.* 228–30); treading the carpets in a symbolic reenactment of the sacrifice, he discounts the verbal omen again (*klêdôn*, 926f.). Cf. *Ch.* 190f. (ἐμὴ δὲ μήτηρ, οὐδαμῶς ἐπώνυμον/ φρόνημα). On *Ch.* 827–30, see R. J. Rabel, *Hermes* 108 (1980) 253–55.

31. For the construction and sense of τούτων . . . ξύμβολα (Ag. 144), see Heinz Neitzel, "Artemis und Agamemnon in der Parodos des Aischyleischen 'Agamemnon,'" *Hermes* 107 (1979) 17. I follow Fraenkel (above, n. 7) 2:88, however, in referring τούτων to the portent and therefore to the war.

32. Fraenkel (above, n. 7) 2:86f., adopts Lachmann's emendation, αἰνεῖ for αἰτεῖ at *Ag.* 144; I follow Neitzel (above, n. 31) 16–17 and n. 43, retaining αἰτεῖ.

33. Cf. also the suggestion of violence in Agamemnon's description of healing, 848–50; cf. Heraclitus, frr. 58, 111.

34. If Apollo is the "destroyer," of course, the herald's premise is mistaken: cf. *Ag.* 55–59, *Ch.* 151.

35. For Heraclitus also, the complex structure of the world makes the name "Zeus" inadequate as a sign of its ruling principle (fr. 32); in particular, if "Zeus" (genitive *Zênos*) signifies "life" (cf. *zên*), the unity of life and death is obscured when life is named as primary. (However, Kirk [above, n. 20] 392, does not find a significant etymology here.) For the definition of Zeus in Aeschylus and Heraclitus, cf. Burkhard Gladigow, "Aischylos und Heraklit," *Archiv für Geschichte der Philosophie* 44 (1962) 225–39. For the sense of *Ag.* 160–66, see Lebeck (above, n. 8) 22–24; for the Heraclitean affinity of the passage, cf. Rösler (above, n. 17) 13 n. 33.

36. The two figures are sometimes difficult to distinguish: a metaphor will seem oxymoronic if its component terms are polar or nearly so; cf. n. 42 below.

37. See Lebeck (above, n. 8) 74, on the carpet scene, for example.

38. Men, of course, do not look like beasts, and this is part of the sense of *dipous*, *Ag.* 1258.

39. When Clytemnestra calls Cassandra's death an "extra dish" (1447), she complicates the moral significance of her deed in the same way.

40. At *Ag.* 1387, according to Fraenkel (above, n. 7) 3:652, "Enger's Διός is clearly right." For the definition of metaphor here, cf. Arist. *Poetics* 1457b6–7: μεταφορὰ δέ ἐστιν ὀνόματος ἀλλοτρίου ἐπιφορά.

41. *Ag.* 182: βιαίως codd: βίαιος Turnebus; with the adverbial form, of course, there is no metaphor. For chthonic *kharis*, cf. *Ag.* 1385–87, *Eu.* 253.

42. Perhaps a broken definition produces an enlarged one (if *kharis* is not *kharis*, why should it not be *biaios*?) or the reverse; see also *Ch.* 504 (if Agamemnon is "not dead, having died," then Orestes may become

metaphorically identified as "Agamemnon"). In either case, the logic of the oxymoron and metaphor is consistent, and their effects are complementary.

43. See Lebeck (above, n. 8) 50, on the equation of the Furies' agents, for example.

44. Cf. W. B. Stanford, *Aeschylus in His Style* (Dublin, 1942) 136.

45. See Lebeck (above, n. 8) 34, 176 n. 19, and William Whallon, "Why is Artemis Angry?" *AJP* 82 (1961) 83 and n. 19. For a narrower reading, based upon a different view of the force of figurative language, cf. Michael Gagarin, *Aeschylean Drama* (Berkeley and Los Angeles, 1976) 63f.

46. Cf. Lebeck (above, n. 8) 33: the two principles coincide here, as they do in the sacrifice of Iphigenia. For Orestes and his family, cf. *Ch.* 1016f.

47. Cf. R. F. Goheen, "Aspects of Dramatic Symbolism: Three Studies in the *Oresteia*," *AJP* 76 (1955) 113–37, reprinted in *Aeschylus: A Collection of Critical Essays*, ed. M. H. McCall (Englewood Cliffs, N.J., 1972) 117.

48. *Eu.* 69f: αἷς οὐ μείγνυται / θεῶν τις οὐδ᾽ ἄνθρωπος οὐδὲ θήρ ποτε; cf. 386, 721f., and Fraenkel ad *Ag.* 637. This is of course a change for the better: the association between chthonic and Olympian deities in the *Agamemnon* hinders, rather than foreshadows, the resolution of their conflict in the *Eumenides* because resolution cannot be achieved until the parties of the conflict are distinctly defined. For a different view, see Lebeck (above, n. 8) 64.

49. Cf. *Ag.* 1580 for binding and the Furies in the murder of Agamemnon.

50. For the metaphor elsewhere in the trilogy and for the Furies' unique status here, see Froma Zeitlin, "The Motif of the Corrupted Sacrifice in Aeschylus' *Oresteia*," *TAPA* 96 (1965) 485; for an intermediate stage in the metaphor's obsolescence, see 497.

51. It is therefore not necessary for Athena to give the Furies a new name, Eumenides (Kindly Ones), although it is possible that she does so, perhaps in a lost passage following *Eu.* 1027: cf. the play's *hypothesis* and Harpocr. s.v. Εὐμενίδες.

52. Thomson (above, n. 15) 286, translates *Eu.* 554 "with a cargo of possessions in which all distinctions of right and wrong are confounded."

53. The word means "evil daughters" (*schlimme Töchter*) according to Detlev Fehling, "ΝΥΚΤΟΣ ΠΑΙΔΕΣ ΑΠΑΙΔΕΣ Α. Eum. 1034 und das sogenannte Oxymoron in der Tragödie," *Hermes* 96 (1968) 142–55, but his detailed argument somehow overlooks the essential point, that the Furies cannot be so named by a chorus enjoining "euphemism"; for *apais* as "childless," cf. *Ag.* 753. For the sense of the passage, see Lebeck (above, n. 8) 133.

54. Cf. Zeitlin (above, n. 50) 507.

55. For the problem of defining Zeus, cf. Aesch. frr. 92 N^2 = 317 M, 70 N^2 = 105 M; *Supp.* 93–95. For Hades, cf. Heraclitus fr. 15.

56. Cf. E. R. Dodds, "Morals and Politics in the *Oresteia,*" *PCPS* 186 (1960) 27; Albin Lesky, "Decision and Responsibility in the Tragedy of Aeschylus," *JHS* 86 (1966) 82; J. D. Denniston and Denys Page, eds., *Aeschylus: Agamemnon* (Oxford, 1957; repr. 1960) xxvii–xxviii; N. G. L. Hammond, "Personal Freedom and Its Limitations in the *Oresteia,*" *JHS* 85 (1965) 42–55; H. D. F. Kitto, *Form and Meaning in Drama* (London, 1956; paper ed., London and New York, 1960) 3–6.

57. Affective and cognitive apprehension are merged in the psychology of "magical" communication. For a related problem, cf. von Fritz (above, n. 28) 83–85.

58. Cf. Lebeck (above, n. 8) 52, for the language of the *Agamemnon* as a *pathos,* followed by *mathos;* according to the argument given here, however, the listener's *pathos* and *mathos* come simultaneously, for understanding consists in nothing other than the "experience" of speech.

59. Hesiod's Muses, of course, enable their audience to forget its own, personal trouble (cf. *Th.* 55, 98–103); Aeschylus releases his audience from cares imposed by the drama itself.

CHAPTER FIVE

1. Cratylus, in Plato's *Cratylus,* seems to entertain such notions; see G. S. Kirk, "The Problem of the *Cratylus,*" *AJP* 72 (1951) 239f., on the possibility that his theory of language is derived from early magical beliefs.

2. Cf. *On Nature* 77–82, for the independence of *phronoumena.*

3. Compare the notion of a mental image derived from speech, which Plutarch ascribes to Simonides; see F. A. Yates, *The Art of Memory* (Chicago and London, 1966; repr. paper ed., 1974) 28.

4. See, for example, Jacqueline de Romilly, "Gorgias et le pouvoir de la poésie," *JHS* 93 (1973) 155, 161.

5. For the later use of this metaphor, see Elaine Fantham, "Imitation and Evolution: The Discussion of Rhetorical Imitation in Cicero *De Oratore* 2.87–97 and Some Related Problems of Ciceronian Theory," *CP* 73 (1978) 12 n. 34, and R. P. McKeon, "Literary Criticism and the Concept of Imitation in Antiquity," *Modern Philology* 34 (1936), reprinted in *Critics and Criticism,* ed. R. S. Crane, paper ed. (Chicago and London, 1952) 126f.

6. For the dates of Gorgias and Damon, see C. P. Segal, "Gorgias and the Psychology of the Logos," *HSCP* 66 (1962) 150 n. 103; for the theo-

ries of Damon, see W. D. Anderson, *Ethos and Education in Greek Music* (Cambridge, Mass., 1966).

7. See above, chapter 3, passim.

8. For a natural correspondence between words and psychic things (beliefs, feelings, perceptions) rather than objective ones, cf. Arist. *de Int.* 16a4, and Phillip DeLacey, "The Epicurean Analysis of Language," *AJP* 60 (1939) 88f. and n. 13.

9. See *Helen* 8, where "persuade" and "deceive" indifferently describe the same process, and *Helen* 10, for "persuade" and "enchant."

10. This distinction between the Gorgianic view and the one found in *Dissoi Logoi* and *Vit. Aesch.* is noted by T. G. Rosenmeyer, "Gorgias, Aeschylus, and *Apate*," *AJP* 76 (1955) 234f. and n. 33; cf. de Romilly (above, n. 4) 160.

11. Plato distinguishes these as degrees of mimesis at *Rep.* 392d–394c but seems to discount the importance of the distinction at 602b8–10; cf. 607a for Homer as a tragedian, and 379a, where the same standards are applied to epic, melic, and tragic poetry.

12. For the connections between Gorgias and Aristophanes, see Max Pohlenz, "Die Anfänge der griechischen Poetik," *NGG* (1920) 142–78, reprinted in *Kleine Schriften*, ed. Heinrich Dörrie (Hildesheim, 1965) 2:436–72, especially 453–56, and Segal (above, n. 6) 130 and n. 111; Rudolf Pfeiffer, *History of Classical Scholarship* (Oxford, 1968) 46f., takes a sceptical view. On *ekplêxis*, see also W. J. Verdenius, "Gorgias' Doctrine of Deception," in *The Sophists and Their Legacy*, ed. G. B. Kerferd, Hermes Einzelschriften 44 (Wiesbaden, 1981) 120 n. 25. At most, it is Gorgianic theory and not Gorgias himself that is associated with Aeschylus in the *Frogs*. Aristophanes seems to have treated Gorgias elsewhere as a Euripidean figure, the type of the professional rhetor and a master of the tongue; cf. *Birds* 1701.

13. I follow Ludwig Radermacher, ed., *Aristophanes' 'Frösche,'* 2d ed. (Vienna, 1954), in taking φωτός as Euripides and ἀνδρός as Aeschylus at 820 (262) and in assigning πλευμόνων πολὺν πόνον to Aeschylus at 829 (263). But cf. C. P. Segal, "The Character and Cult of Dionysus and the Unity of the *Frogs*," *HSCP* 65 (1961) 223.

14. Another notion, possibly related to this one, is exploited by Aristophanes for comic effect in the *Frogs* and explicitly stated at *Thesm.* 167: poetry must resemble the poet's own nature (ὅμοια γὰρ ποιεῖν ἀνάγκη τῇ φύσει). See Rosemary Harriott, *Poetry and Criticism before Plato* (London, 1969) 137f. and, for the later influence of the notion, M. R. Lefkowitz, "The Poet as Hero: Fifth Century Autobiography and Subsequent Biographical Fiction," *CQ* ns 28 (1978) 459–69.

15. Because Aeschylus confronts an alien point of view here, he must express as a rule what he might otherwise regard as a natural tendency: hence, ἀνάγκη (1058).

16. *Frogs* 52–67; for the difficulty in defining Dionysus's desire, cf. the difficulty in locating his heart (482–85). On the question of Dionysus's sensibilities, see Segal (above, n. 13) passim, especially 210f.

17. For Dionysus's pleasure, see 1413: τὸν μὲν γὰρ ἡγοῦμαι σοφὸν τῷ δ' ἥδομαι. Radermacher (above, n. 13) 335, identifies the former as Euripides, the latter as Aeschylus.

18. *Helen* 10, 13; in *Helen* 5, pleasure is associated specifically with the unfamiliar. Cf. Segal (above, n. 6) 122–24.

19. Cf. the use of τίκτειν (1059) and the comments of Harriott (above, n. 14) 151.

20. λαλιὰν . . . καὶ στωμυλίαν, 1069; cf. 1071, 1160, 954; for the living poets, cf. 91. For old-fashioned speech as the call for food and the chant of men rowing, see 1072f.; cf. *Clouds* 1002ff., 1052–54.

21. The chant is ῥυππαπαῖ (1073), which may be compared to the Frogs' croaking (209f., e.g.) and Euripides' parody of Aeschylean non-sensical repetition, τοφλαττοθρατ τοφλαττοθρατ (1285–95).

22. For Aeschylus's effort to produce the effect of the chant, cf. 1021f., 1025–27.

23. On the sexual connotations of Euripides' losing his ληκύθιον, see C. H. Whitman, "ΛΗΚΥΘΙΟΝ ΑΠΩΛΕΣΕΝ," *HSCP* 73 (1969) 109–12; J. G. Griffith, "Ληκύθιον ἀπώλεσεν: A postscript," *HSCP* 74 (1970) 43–44; and Bruno Snell, "Lekythion," *Hermes* 107 (1979) 129–33.

24. This sort of precision must be distinguished from Protagoras's *orthoepeia* and from the etymological practices of the *Cratylus*; see Pfeiffer (above, n. 12) 280 and C. J. Classen, "The Study of Language amongst Socrates' Contemporaries," in *Sophistik*, ed. C. J. Classen, Wege der Forschung 187 (Darmstadt, 1976) 231. Prodicus, rather than Protagoras, is probably the model for Euripides here, according to Pfeiffer, 39f.; cf. Pohlenz (above, n. 12) 440; Classen, 224 and 230; C. P. Segal, "Protagoras' *Orthoepeia* in Aristophanes' Battle of the Prologues," *RhM* 113 (1970) 158–62. At *Frogs* 1182–97, it appears that Euripides' own use of words cannot stand too close an examination, but the standard applied here is nevertheless his.

25. Cf. Gorgias *Helen* 16 and τερατεύεσθαι at *Frogs* 834, 925; *Knights* 624ff.

26. βιβλίον τ' ἔχων ἕκαστος μανθάνει τὰ δεξιά (1114). For Euripides as *dexios*, cf. 71, 540f. (Theramenes, Euripides' pupil, 967); for Euripides and books, cf. 943, 1409. Prodicus, the teacher of semantic precision, is associated with the book in fr. 490. See also J. D. Denniston, "Technical Terms in Aristophanes," *CQ* 21 (1927) 113–21, especially 117–19.

27. Cf. Cratinus fr. 122 and *Clouds* 961–1023 for old-fashioned hostility toward books. On the extent of literacy, cf. Leonard Woodbury, "Aristophanes' *Frogs* and Athenian Literacy: *Ran.* 52–53, 1114," *TAPA* 106 (1976) 349–57. Ambitious attempts to relate literacy to a wide range of

cultural phenomena are found in Eric Havelock, *Preface to Plato* (Oxford, 1963) and Jack Goody and Ian Watt, "The Consequences of Literacy," in *Literacy in Traditional Societies*, ed. Jack Goody (Cambridge, 1968) 27–68.

28. Cf. Havelock (above, n. 27) 129 n. 6, 189. Since the use of an alphabet requires an analytical approach toward the sounds of language, it is not surprising to find that Hippias may have undertaken such a program; see 86A11 DK[8] and Giuliana Lanata, *Poetica pre-platonica* (Florence, 1963) 210ff.

29. Madness and inspiration are contrasted with Lysias's written speech (*Phdr.* 244ff., 243c), sincerity (*Phdr.* 276c) with writing (παιδίας χάριν, 276d).

30. For ethics and law in oral versus literate culture, cf. Plut. *Lyc.* 13, cited by C. P. Roth, "The Kings and the Muses in Hesiod's *Theogony*," *TAPA* 106 (1976) 336.

31. See Hjalmar Frisk, *Griechisches Etymologisches Wörterbuch* (Heidelberg, 1970), s.v. ψυχή.

32. This civic theme pervades the *Frogs*: cf. 798 (where μειαγωγήσουσι suggests that tragedy is tested as though it were being enrolled in the lists of citizens), 686f. (for the function of Aristophanes' own chorus), 1419 (where saving the city is equated with preserving its ability to present choruses). Cf. Segal (above, n. 13) and C. H. Whitman, *Aristophanes and the Comic Hero* (Cambridge, Mass., 1964) chapt. 7 passim.

33. Aeschylus associates himself with the culture of the gymnasium at 1069–72, 1087f.

34. Cf. n. 5 above and Plato *Rep.* 379a for (τύποι) ἐν οἷς δεῖ μυθολογεῖν τοὺς ποιητάς.

35. The process mentioned by Plato (*Prot.* 326a) and Isocrates (4.159) seems to be different, however.

36. Cf. Radermacher (above, n. 13) 295f. and, for the notion that the quality of poetic language is defined by the quality of the actions it describes, cf. Pindar *N* 5, discussed above in chapter 3.

37. Cf. the Pindaric *kairos* discussed above in chapter 3.

38. Both may perhaps be regarded as aspects of realism: see Anderson (above, n. 6) 52; cf. Plato *Rep.* 397.

39. See Radermacher (above, n. 13) 323, on δωδεκαμήχανος and cf. Euripides' Muse (1306–8).

40. Cf. Ps.-Xen. *Ath. Pol.* 1.10–12; for the significance of Xanthias's role as an upstart slave in the *Frogs*, see Whitman (above, n. 32) 237f. and Segal (above, n. 13) 216f.

41. Cf. *Acharn.* 634; *Knights* 633.

42. With Aeschylus ἐριβρεμέτας who ἐτερατεύετο his audience (814, 834), cf. *Acharn.* 530f. (ὀργῇ Περικλέης οὐλύμπιος/ ἤστραπτ' ἐβρόντα ξυνεκύκα τὴν Ἑλλάδα) and *Knights* 626f. (on Cleon, ὁ δ' ἄρ' ἔνδον ἐλασ-

ἰβροντ' ἀναρρηγνὺς ἔπη/ τερατευόμενος). For the confusion induced by the war and the war party, cf. *Knights* 692, 431; *Peace* 320, 270.

43. According to Aeschylus, poets were the first to teach men the arts of civilization (1030-36); the catalogue he gives seems to be conventional: cf. Hippias, fr. 6.

44. Cf. the unifying effects of the chant.

45. Cf. *Clouds* 1400 for the conflict between the new arts and κα-θεστῶτες νόμοι.

46. Cf. *Frogs* 360.

47. *Frogs* 1463-65. The policy also recalls Themistocles' during the Persian War, seventy-five years earlier, and its antiquity no doubt reflects Aeschylus's feeling that only one thing is good, and good for Athens, and so it need never be questioned or changed. On the practical implausibility of Aeschylus's advice, cf. Whitman (above, n. 32) 255. For a different account, see A. H. Sommerstein, "Aristophanes, *Frogs* 1463-5," *CQ* 58 (1974) 24-27.

48. The inconsequence noted here, as well as other difficulties, can be repaired by wholesale emendation of the text: see below, n. 58. It should be apparent, however, that if Aeschylus's Periclean policy fits well with his Periclean use of language, there is no obvious reason to delete 1463-65: cf. Garry Wills, "Aeschylus' Victory in the *Frogs*," *AJP* 90 (1969) 53 n. 6; Heinrich Dörrie, "Aristophanes' Frösche 1433-67," *Hermes* 84 (1956) 312-15, retains the passage.

49. He was not involved in the revolution of 411: καὶ γὰρ οὐκ ἐπι-τήδειον αὐτὸν εἶναι ἐς ὀλιγαρχίαν ἐλθεῖν (Thuc. 8.63.4; cf. 8.68.3, 8.81).

50. Cf. Plato *Rep.* 545b-c.

51. B. M. W. Knox, *Oedipus at Thebes*, paper ed. (New Haven and London, 1957) 64, cites Cratinus fr. 240 and Plut. *Per.* 39.

52. Herodotus 6.131 and Plut. *Per.* 3; cf. the story of Cypselus (Herodotus 5.92.2), and, for Aristophanes' familiarity with Herodotus, see Gennaro Perrotta, "Erodoto Parodiato da Aristofane," *Rendiconti del Istituto delle Scienze e Lettere* 59 (1926) 105-14. Cf. Whitman (above, n. 32) 254, for another explanation of the lion cub.

53. *Knights* 1037ff.

54. The ξενικοὶ λόγοι of *Acharn.* 634 may be Gorgias's, according to Victor Ehrenberg, *The People of Aristophanes* (Oxford, 1943; repr. London and New York, 1974), 279f.

55. Cf. *Knights* 431; *Peace* 320. For the *tyrannis* of Zeus in Aristophanes, see *Plutus* 124; *Birds* 1605, 1643, 1673, 1708. Also, for a possible link between *PB* and the *Birds*, see C. J. Herington, "A Study in the *Prometheia*. Part II: *Birds* and *Prometheia*," *Phoenix* 17 (1963) 236-43, especially 239.

56. For the tyrannical quality of Gorgianic rhetoric, see Segal (above,

158 NOTES TO PAGES 95-99

n. 6) 148 n. 87. Aristotle (*Pol.* 1313a9) regards *apatê* as a definitive quality of tyranny.

57. Cf. Whitman (above, n. 32) 244, 252f., 256.

58. Radermacher (above, n. 13) 244f., among others, would remove this impression by deleting 1442–50 and 1460–66. But there is no reason to assume, as he does, that Euripides cannot give the same advice as Aeschylus, that Aristophanes prefers Aeschylus and so Euripides must seem foolish, or that Aeschylus would not bargain for his own interest, and so there is no sure basis for emending the text here (cf. n. 48). And if the text is corrupt, but the corruption arose from an original confusion produced by genuine signs of Aristophanes' ambivalent attitude toward the tragedians, emendation directed toward clarity and simplicity (or Dörrie's "stärkere Kontraste" [above, n. 48] 315) will surely be mistaken.

59. If there is any synthesis here, it is negative, for Alcibiades may represent the vices of the two tragedians: he belongs not only to the class of would-be tyrants but also to the modern Socratic set; like Euripides, he is talkative and effeminate (*Acharn.* 716).

60. Cf. the opening of the play, where Dionysus raises (and drops) the question of purified humor.

61. χρῶμαι γὰρ αὐτοῦ τοῦ στόματος τῷ στρογγύλῳ./ τοὺς νοῦς δ' ἀγοραίους ἧττον ἢ 'κεῖνος ποιῶ. αὐτοῦ is identified as Euripides by the two sources of the fragment (schol. Plat. Clark. 330 Bekk.; Plut. *Mor.* 30d); for ἀγοραῖος, cf. *Frogs* 1013–15.

62. Cf. Segal (above, n. 13) passim.

63. Cf. θειότατα ἔργα, Gorgias *Helen* 8.

64. Literally, "if the story is clear" (εἰ σαφὴς οὗτος λόγος).

65. More might be made of 308–10 if the passage were not corrupt; see A. M. Dale, *Euripides: Helen* (Oxford, 1967) ad loc.

66. For the Greeks' treatment of single words with multiple referents, see Ernst Heitsch, *Die Entdeckung der Homonymie*, Akademie der Wissenschaften und der Literatur, Mainz: Abhandlungen der geistes- und sozialwissenschaftlichen Klasse, 11 (Mainz, 1972), especially 501–12, 518–25.

67. See W. K. C. Guthrie, *A History of Greek Philosophy*, vol. 3 (Cambridge, 1969); pt. 1 repr. as *The Sophists*, paper ed. (1971) 180. For the appearance of the theory and technique of probable argument in Athens, see George Kennedy, *The Art of Persuasion in Greece* (Princeton, 1963) 30f.

68. According to the metaphor of the *Helen*, however, which makes Egypt the underworld (see discussion later in this chapter), Menelaus is equivocally dead when he arrives there.

69. For "clarity" and truth, cf. Knox (above, n. 51) 133 and 243 n. 89.

70. For the *onoma*, cf. Friedrich Solmsen, "*Onoma* and *pragma* in Euripides' *Helen*," *CR* 48 (1934) 119–21.

71. The treatment of the *eidôlon* given here is largely derived from J. P. Vernant, "Figuration de l'invisible et catégorie psychologique du double: Le colossos," in *Mythe et pensée chez les Grecs* (Paris, 1965) 251–64.

72. For the presence of an *agalma* as equivalent to the presence of a god, cf., e.g., Aesch. *Eu.* 55f.

73. Cf. *Alc.* 354–56 and Homer *Il.* 23.99–107.

74. Eur. fr. 971; *Or.* 1086f.; *Supp.* 531–4, 1140–42. See also Erwin Rohde, *Psyche*, trans. W. B. Hillis (London, 1925; repr. paper ed., New York, 1966) 461 n. 146.

75. *Helen* 243f.; cf. *Hom. h. Dem.* 5–8, 425–33.

76. Something like an inversion of underworld and world above accounts for Helen's living presence in the house of Plutus, and when Menelaus demands (969–74) that he and his wife be freed or else that all the dead of Troy return to life, he acknowledges this inversion; if it is not corrected in one way, then it must be corrected in another. Cf. A. N. Pippin, "Euripides' *Helen*: A Comedy of Ideas," *CP* 55 (1960) 156, from which this argument is taken.

77. Cf. Vernant (above, n. 71) 256.

78. Isocrates 3.7; for the assumption, cf. chapter 1.

79. *Aithêr*, as the basic element of divine substances, is equated allegorically with Zeus: cf. frr. 941, 985; *Ion* 1078f.

80. It is treated differently, however, in fr. 1018 and *Tr.* 884–87. For the arguments that follow here, cf. A. P. Burnett, *Catastrophe Survived* (Oxford, 1971) 95f. and Pippin (above, n. 76) 158–61.

81. Cf. Richard Kannicht, *Euripides: Helena* (Heidelberg, 1969) 2:261.

82. For a "genuine" (*gnêsiê*) *gnômê*, independent of the senses, cf. Democritus 68B11; for the divinity of *gnômê*, Heraclitus 22B78; for *gnômê* as linked to knowledge of the universe's secret working, Heraclitus 22B41. According to G. S. Kirk's interpretation of fr. 41, *gnômê* is an internal object of *epistasthai*, and so it may be identified with such knowledge; see *Heraclitus: The Cosmic Fragments* (Cambridge, 1954) 388f. For fifth-century views of the *gnômê*, see Knox (above, n. 51) 124 and 240 n. 59.

83. See Burnett (above, n. 80) 95.

84. Since this process begins with the departure of the *eidôlon*, it is tempting to suppose that its disappearance entails something more than a narrative convenience, namely, Helen's recovery of her divine ethereal self, which has hitherto been separated from her so that it might do Zeus's work at Troy. For the *eidôlon* as an immortal and divine organ of knowledge, like the Euripidean *gnômê*, cf. Pindar fr. 116 Bowra = 131b Sn-M.

85. For poetic artfulness as a theme in the play, cf. Burnett (above, n.80) 91f.; Pippin (above, n. 76) 152, 154; C. P. Segal, "The Two Worlds of Euripides' 'Helen,'" *TAPA* 102 (1971) 553–614, especially 610–12.

86. Cf. fr. 192, where the *pneuma* of the gods is identified as the source

of poetry, and *Helen* 865–67, where *pneuma* and *aithêr* are linked.

87. For the *gnômê* as the poet's active organ, cf. *Medea* 424f.

88. Or, "in grief, unforgetting"; see Dale (above, n. 65) ad 1337.

89. Cf. *Hom. h. Asclepius* 16.4.

90. *Hom. h. Aphr.* 33–39. For sex and *thelxis*, cf. *Il.* 14.215; Aesch. *Supp.* 1034–42; Bacchylides 5.175; Soph. *Trach.* 354f.; Eur. *Hipp.* 1274; *Bacch.* 404.

91. *Hom. h. Dem.* 393–403.

92. Thus, the return of Kore is conflated with the interlude at Eleusis: cf. *Hom. h. Dem.* 192–205.

93. The two divine acts are complementary and symmetrical, for Zeus saves the human race by sending Aphrodite to the Mother and reduces it by sending the *eidôlon* to Troy: cf. *Helen* 39f. Underlying Euripides' alteration of the Eleusinian myth may be a glimmer of the idea that Kore's incomplete, partial release from the underworld is itself only half of the palpable satisfaction the mother seeks; thus, her daughter will belong both to life and death, like an *eidôlon*, the living double of someone who is dead.

94. Cf. chapter 2.

95. Cf. chapter 3.

CHAPTER SIX

1. See above, chapters 1, 2, and 3.

2. Frr. 910, 911, and 1023 N^2 are assigned to the *Antiope* by T. B. L. Webster, *The Tragedies of Euripides* (London, 1967) 207. He cites 1023 as 182a; for its place in the *Antiope*, see also Philostr. *Imag.* 1, 10.

3. Cf. E. R. Dodds, ed., *Plato: Gorgias* (Oxford, 1959) 275f.

4. The lesson might also have come from the more recent example of Phrynichus's *Capture of Miletus*. For the limits of enchantment in Homer, see chapter 1. In fr. 202, Badham's conjecture (νοεῖ for νοσεῖ, cited by Nauck) would make the limitation of Amphion's subject matter more radical.

5. Fr. 188; cf. fr. 185. Historically, this omission corresponds to the program of a post-Homeric muse, who celebrates the marriages of the gods instead of human battles: cf. Stesichorus 210 *PMG*. An erotic muse replaces the martial one in Anacreon fr. eleg. 2 West: cf. the two topics of song in *Hom. h. Apollo* 186ff.

6. This image makes explicit what was implicit in Hesiod's account of song: see chapter 2.

7. Frr. 11, 12 DK[8]. For Amphion's similar sentiment, see fr. 210; cf. *Ion* 338–41; *HF* 1340–46.

8. Earth seems to have been regarded as a primary substance by

Xenophanes, Theagenes' contemporary (frr. 27, 33 DK[8]). Félix Buffière, *Les mythes d'Homère et la pensée grecque* (Paris, 1956) 101–22, taking the Venetus B Scholium to *Il.* 20.67 as a starting point, discusses the early origins of the notion Zeus = *aithêr* and its possible influence upon allegorists. See also Giuliana Lanata, *Poetica pre-platonica* (Florence, 1963) 106–11 and Michael Murrin, *The Allegorical Epic* (Chicago and London, 1980) 8f.

9. Fr. 1023 N[2]. Webster (above, n. 2) suggests that fr. 941 also belongs in this context. Cf. fr. 985; *Ion* 1078f.; and chapter 5 for Euripides and *aithêr*.

10. For the equivalence of poetry and philosophy, cf. *Alc.* 962–66.

11. According to Webster (above, n. 2), fr. 910 might naturally follow the performance of Amphion's song.

12. For the notion of enchantment in the fifth century, see chapter 5.

13. For the identity of these poets, see Denys Page, ed., *Euripides: Medea* (Oxford, 1938; repr. 1964) ad 191.

14. With this statement, the nurse seems to associate herself with Hesiod's uninitiated shepherds, "bellies only" who know nothing of the Muses' gift (*Th.* 26), men who eat but cannot sing.

15. For the possibility that Zethus favors some form of poetry, see Dodds (above, n. 3) 278f. ad *Gorgias* 486c4–8.

16. See chapter 5.

17. See chapter 5 n. 90 and section on Euripides' *Helen*; cf. *Bacch.* 404f.; Aesch. *Supp.* 1034–40.

18. This is the interpretation of Page (above, n. 13) ad 439. Cf. the *kharis* of *aidôs*, *IA* 563–67.

19. Thus, Aphrodite is conventionally associated with the Graces: see *Il.* 5.338; *Od.* 18.193f., 8.362–66; *Cypria* fr. 3 Kinkel; *Hom. h. Aphr.* 58–63; Pindar *Paean* 6.3f. Aphrodite seems to be interchangeable with one of the Graces at *Il.* 18.382f. and Hes. *Th.* 945f.; cf. *Od.* 8.266ff.

20. For a more explicit treatment of Aphrodite's double influence upon social behavior, see Pindar *N* 8 and chapter 3.

21. For the genealogy, see Page (above, n. 13) ad loc.

22. Amphion too sees a social benefit in enchantment and therefore in poetry: temperate men make steadfast friends (fr. 194); men who have surrendered themselves to the enjoyment of palpable, ephemeral things make bad citizens (fr. 201). Cf. fr. 910: contemplation of "immortal nature's ageless order" prevents immoral behavior. For the social significance of "musical" harmony, see chapter 3 on Pindar *Pythia* 1.

23. See chapter 5 on the *Helen*.

24. Hesiod, *Th.* 102f., e.g.

25. Cf. fr. 200. However, it is not clear whether Amphion speaks these verses; fr. 185 suggests that he does not.

26. See chapter 3.

27. Cf. Pindar *O* 9.27f.; Eur. *Helen* 1341–5, and Rosemary Harriott, *Poetry and Criticism before Plato* (London, 1969) 125f.

28. Cf. nn. 17 and 18 above.

29. Cf. Ulrich von Wilamowitz-Moellendorff, ed., *Euripides: Herakles*, 2d ed. (Berlin, 1933) 358f. ad loc.

30. The chorus's joy will be confounded after a short interval, when Heracles murders his wife and children; the song, which praises Heracles for *areta* "exceeding his birth" as Zeus's son, is a foil for the hero's downfall, which demonstrates the superior power of gods. For this pattern of joyful lyric anticipation and confounding dramatic event, cf. Soph. *Ajax* 692–718 and the death of Ajax.

31. Cf. Amphitryon's complaint (339–47). The old men judge the gods in the same way that they judge Heracles, according to present utility (cf. 655–59, 757–59), and in this respect they may be distinguished from the poet of frr. 910 and 1023 N^2, who worships gods who are admirable because of their difference (and distance) from human beings. The religious controversy surfaces in the encounter between Theseus and Heracles: see *HF* 1313–21, 1340–46.

32. For the connection between this passage and the encomiastic ode for Heracles, cf. κύκνος ὣς (692) and πολιὸς ὄρνις (110); and for these images, see James Diggle, ed., *Euripides: Phaethon* (Cambridge, 1970) 104 ad 78; cf. *IT* 1104f.

33. The chorus claims no enchanting power for the song with which it commemorates Heracles' virtue when it believes that Heracles is dead: this song is a dirge rather than a celebration, a symbolic measure of lost felicity rather than an intrinsic source of present strength or joy; see 348–58.

34. The chorus's song differs fundamentally from Pindar's because it is explicitly a human thing like the *areta* it celebrates, a blessing contrived by men as a replacement for youth, which the gods would have given had they the insight and the art (*xunesis kai sophia*) of human beings; see 655–72.

35. Judged in this way, the chorus's song falls short of Euripides' play to the extent that Euripides illuminates Heracles's virtue even when it is contradicted by worldly circumstance, when Heracles has fallen into dishonor for having murdered his family. At least part of the charm Heracles retains in dishonor (as Euripides represents him) comes from his stubborn adherence to principle, for example, the unworldly purity of his belief in gods as beings wholly unlike men.

36. For reading and disenchantment, see chapter 5 on the *Frogs*.

37. Cf. Teiresias's interpretation of Dionysian legend in *Bacch*. 272–97 and the comments of E. R. Dodds, *Euripides: Bacchae*, 2d ed. (Oxford, 1960) ad loc.

38. Cf. the sophist Antiphon, DK⁸ 87B44 frag. A col. 3, 25–col. 4, 8.

39. Cf. Felix Heinimann, *Nomos und Phusis* (Basel, 1965) 43–56.

40. According to the interpretation of W. S. Barrett, ed., *Euripides: Hippolytus* (Oxford, 1964) ad loc.

41. Barrett (above, n. 40) ad loc. For the nurse's reliance upon authority, cf. 266.

42. Cf. Theseus's argument (*HF* 1313–21).

43. The chastity of life in the meadow is its more obvious quality, but it need not for this reason be regarded as irrelevant to Phaedra's imagined release there. However, cf. B. M. W. Knox, "The *Hippolytus* of Euripides," *YCS* 13 (1952) 6; C. P. Segal, "The Tragedy of the *Hippolytus*: The Waters of Ocean and the Untouched Meadow," *HSCP* 70 (1965) 124f.; and J. M. Bremer, "The Meadow of Love and Two Passages in Euripides' *Hippolytus*," *Mnem.* 28 (1975) 268–80.

44. For enchantment and death, cf. chapter 1 on the Sirens and chapter 5 on Eur. *Helen*.

45. In this respect, the meadow recalls *areta* and poetry as Pindar values these things, for *areta* grows like a plant fed by wisdom (*N* 8.40–42), a product of nature like the poetry that praises it, distinct from the forced, impious success of men who use learning (cf. *O* 2.86).

46. Or, the chorus's own piety by itself provides the comfort, perhaps a more exact parallel to Hippolytus's experience. For interpretation of the passage, cf. Barrett (above, n. 40) ad loc.

47. Cf. Denys Page, ed., *Sappho and Alcaeus* (Oxford, 1955) 37 ad loc.

48. Threnos VII (frr. 129, 131a, 130) Maehler = 114–116 Bowra = Plut. *consol. ad Apoll.* 35 p. 120c. According to Alexander Turyn, "The Sapphic Ostracon," *TAPA* 73 (1942) 308–18, Pindar's paradise is Orphic and indicates an Orphic source for Sappho's fr. 2, but it seems more likely that the Orphic element, if any, is itself derived from an earlier, perhaps literary source; cf. Thomas McEvilley, "Sappho, Fragment Two," *Phoenix* 26 (1972) 327–31. Perhaps an Orphic association might attach itself subsequently to the description of such places: for the (hostile) suspicion that Hippolytus engages in Orphic practices, cf. 952–54. (The question Barrett addresses ad loc. is different: Hippolytus may display some affinity for Orphic attitudes even if he does not follow Orphic practices consistently.) For the common (and vain) promise of an escape from necessity in poetry and Orphism, cf. *Alc.* 962–71.

49. Cf. also the Graces' *kapon* where the poet dwells (Pindar *O* 9.27); for the intimacy of gods and men in song, cf. Eur. fr. 911.

50. Thus, in the nurse's terms, Hippolytus is "dangerously in love with this thing that shines on earth" (193f.), but the earthly thing is at the same time "dearer than living" in the ordinary way.

51. There is also a corollary problem, the actual relation between the meadow and daily life, and the difference between Artemis and Aphrodite; the structure and the imagery of the play suggest that the meadow

is less exceptional than Hippolytus knows: see the detailed argument of Segal (above, n. 43).

52. Phaedra acknowledges one aspect of this problem, the failure to act in accord with one's moral sensibility (380–84).

53. *Hipp.* 653–55; cf. 1004–6. Cf. Pindar's concern with the double force of *mega eipein*, dangerous speech about dangerous deeds, in N 5, which is discussed above in chapter 3.

54. Cf. chapter 3 on N 8.

55. Cf. the bacchants' pious intolerance. For the space of this single speech at least, Hippolytus has been drawn into a worldly conflict, and he abandons *sôphrosunê*, as E. R. Dodds remarks in "The ΑΙΔΩΣ of Phaedra and the Meaning of the *Hippolytus*," *CR* 39 (1925) 103.

56. See Barrett (above, n. 40) ad 1258f.; cf. 1315–17.

57. *Hipp.* 1403–5: it is possible that Artemis corrects him at 1404, insisting that Phaedra belongs among Aphrodite's pitiable victims; Hippolytus's own statement (1403) ambiguously suggests that Artemis herself has been harmed.

58. Hippolytus discovers two things that keep him rooted in the human condition, an inherited pollution (1379f.) and vulnerability to the gods (which he would like to invert, 1415).

59. Cf. Pietro Pucci, "Euripides: The Monument and the Sacrifice," *Arethusa* 10 (1977) 165–95, especially 184–86.

60. For the myth of Phaethon, see Diggle (above, n. 32) 4–32.

61. Whatever contribution hero-song may have made to the historical development of Attic tragedy (cf. A. W. Pickard-Cambridge, *Dithyramb Tragedy and Comedy*, 2d ed., rev. by T. B. L. Webster [Oxford, 1962] 105–7), it is at least possible that Euripides might imagine himself to be working in the tradition of the choruses who mourned Adrastus at Sicyon (Hdt. 5.67).

ᒉᒉᒉᒉᒉᒉᒉᒉ INDEX ᒉᒉᒉᒉᒉᒉᒉᒉ